W9-CHZ-936

THE CAMP DUTCH OVEN COOKBOOK

The Camp DUTCH OVEN COOKBOOK

Easy 5-Ingredient Recipes to Eat Well in the Great Outdoors

ROBIN DONOVAN

ROCKRIDGE
PRESS

Copyright © 2017 by Robin Donovan

No part of this publication may be reproduced, stored in a retrieval system or transmitted in any form or by any means, electronic, mechanical, photocopying, recording, scanning or otherwise, except as permitted under Sections 107 or 108 of the 1976 United States Copyright Act, without the prior written permission of the Publisher. Requests to the Publisher for permission should be addressed to the Permissions Department, Rockridge Press, 918 Parker St, Suite A-12, Berkeley, CA 94710.

Limit of Liability/Disclaimer of Warranty: The Publisher and the author make no representations or warranties with respect to the accuracy or completeness of the contents of this work and specifically disclaim all warranties, including without limitation warranties of fitness for a particular purpose. No warranty may be created or extended by sales or promotional materials. The advice and strategies contained herein may not be suitable for every situation. This work is sold with the understanding that the publisher is not engaged in rendering medical, legal or other professional advice or services. If professional assistance is required, the services of a competent professional person should be sought. Neither the Publisher nor the author shall be liable for damages arising herefrom. The fact that an individual, organization or website is referred to in this work as a citation and/or potential source of further information does not mean that the author or the Publisher endorses the information the individual, organization or website may provide or recommendations they/it may make. Further, readers should be aware that Internet websites listed in this work may have changed or disappeared between when this work was written and when it is read.

For general information on our other products and services or to obtain technical support, please contact our Customer Care Department within the United States at (866) 744-2665, or outside the U.S. at (510) 253-0500.

Rockridge Press publishes its books in a variety of electronic and print formats. Some content that appears in print may not be available in electronic books, and vice versa.

TRADEMARKS: Rockridge Press and the Rockridge Press logo are trademarks or registered trademarks of Callisto Media Inc. and/or its affiliates, in the United States and other countries, and may not be used without written permission. All other trademarks are the property of their respective owners. Rockridge Press is not associated with any product or vendor mentioned in this book.

Illustrations © Ryan Johnson/Illozoo, 2017

ISBN: Print 978-1-62315-884-2 | eBook 978-1-62315-885-9

FOR CASHEL AND DOUG,
MY FAVORITE CAMPING AND
DINING PARTNERS

Contents

Introduction

I GREW UP IN A "FOODIE" FAMILY. My mother was a great self-taught cook who was always experimenting in the kitchen, drawing culinary inspiration from every corner of the globe. Our home-cooked meals were always interesting and delicious, and we tried every type of restaurant we could find in our diverse area—Thai, Indian, Japanese, Vietnamese, Indonesian, Laotian, Afghani, Persian, Northern Italian, Southern Italian, French, Portuguese, Peruvian, Mexican, and more. We even chose travel destinations based on the food. Ours was a family of adventurous eaters, but no one would have ever called us "outdoorsy." In fact, I never once went camping with my family growing up. I used to joke that my mother thought the only reason a person would camp was if they couldn't afford a hotel room.

Somewhere along the way, outside influences like camping trips with friends' families and sleep-away camp adventures began to sink in, and by the time I was a young adult, I had grown to love camping every bit as much as discovering unfamiliar cuisines. At some point, I even took what was (to me) a big leap: I spent a chunk of my measly paycheck from my first job out of college on a tent, a super warm sleeping bag, and a handful of other camping essentials. I had become a bona fide camping enthusiast. Even so, I was resigned to the misguided belief that camping and eating well didn't go together. Camp cooking was a necessity. It wasn't about making outstanding food. That, I figured, required loads of equipment, long lists of ingredients, intricate timing, and a well-stocked pantry—all things that are sorely lacking at most campsites. My outdoor adventures were fueled by such pedestrian fare as hot dogs, canned baked beans, and quick-cook noodles in a foam cup.

Then came a single camping meal when I was in my mid-20s. I was with a group of friends, and in the evening, we all came together to produce a meal that was both delightfully simple and surprisingly delicious. Everyone contributed to the meal, which included teriyaki chicken kabobs, rice pilaf, grilled asparagus, and more. That evening was a light bulb moment for me, and my approach to cooking was forever changed. Camping meals, I realized, could be every bit as amazing as home-cooked ones. By relying on simple recipes, fresh ingredients, easy techniques, and the most basic equipment, I haven't had to choke down another boring ground beef concoction or dish based on canned cream of mushroom soup. Instead, I've enjoyed everything from fresh-baked Buttery Campfire Beer Bread (page 142) to Spicy Beef and Bean Chili (page 74), Honey-Sweetened Cornbread (page 143), and Pineapple Upside-Down Cake (page 162)—all cooked over a flickering campfire.

Since that night, I've camped—and cooked—at dozens of campsites. What I've learned is that outdoor cooking doesn't need to be elaborate in order to be fantastic. And it doesn't have to rely on processed, canned, or freeze-dried ingredients, either. The truth is, a few good ingredients, simply prepared, can always make a delicious meal—even with only one main cooking vessel: the Dutch oven. Because it is made of cast iron, a Dutch oven is incredibly durable (no worries about damaging it in your travels), great at conducting heat, and versatile enough to cook everything.

A camp-style Dutch oven has legs that enable it to stand over a bed of coals, allowing you to use it like a pot on your kitchen stovetop. You can even control the heat by adding or subtracting briquettes. Another feature of the camp-style Dutch oven is its flat, rimmed lid that is designed to hold hot coals on top. Using this feature, you can approximate the all-around heat of your home oven, again, controlling the heat by the number of hot coals you use. As a result, you can make everything from Cinnamon-Raisin Breakfast Bread Pudding (page 43) to Green Chile and Corn Chowder (page 68), Chicken Braised in Coconut Milk with Basil (page 98), Crusty No-Knead French Bread (page 148), and even desserts like Brown Sugar Berry Crisp (page 156), Double-Chocolate Brownies (page 165), and Quick and Easy Peach Pie (page 159).

Armed with the recipes and advice in this book, a hot fire, and your trusty Dutch oven, you'll soon discover how satisfying campsite-cooked meals can be. The recipes here are simple, none requiring more than five ingredients (not including staples like salt, pepper, butter, and oil), and are easy to prepare. While some recipes might fall back on pantry staples like canned diced tomatoes or broth, none use processed ingredients like canned cream-of-whatever soup, instant ramen noodles, or powdered mixes. All of them draw on fresh, wholesome ingredients, easy techniques, and the genius of the Dutch oven.

There are two things that can always soothe my soul: spending time in the great outdoors and enjoying delicious, wholesome food. I spent too many years thinking these two endeavors were mutually exclusive. Fortunately, I saw that they weren't. With this book, you will, too.

Chapter
One

An Outdoor Cooking Classic

IT'S EASY TO SEE WHY CAST IRON DUTCH OVENS have been a favorite cooking tool, especially for outdoor or fire pit cooking, for centuries. They are capable of producing a huge variety of enticing meals—from breakfasts to stews, main dishes, baked goods, and desserts—with minimal additional equipment. This chapter tells you everything you need to know about camp cooking with a Dutch oven and proves that it is the only pot you need for a delicious camping trip.

The History

Cast iron has virtually always been prized as an ideal material for cooking. Its use as such has been documented as far back as the Han Dynasty in China more than 2,000 years ago. By the sixteenth century, the casting of iron kettles and pots for cooking had taken root throughout Europe, using loam and clay molds to shape the iron. By the early part of the eighteenth century, though, the Dutch emerged as leaders in cast iron cookware production by using molds made of dry sand, which gave their pots a smooth surface that was better for cooking. According to John Ragsdale's book *Dutch Ovens Chronicled*, an Englishman named Abraham Darcy, who learned it from the Dutch, patented this process. Ragsdale theorizes that this is how the pots came to be known as "Dutch ovens." They were soon distributed widely throughout Britain and shipped to its colonies in the Americas.

Though a bit more recent, cast iron cookware's history in the United States is long and storied. First produced in America in 1619, when the first foundry was established, historical documents prove that America's love affair with cast iron Dutch ovens has been hot and heavy ever since.

Take Lewis and Clark and their famous Louisiana Territory expedition early in the nineteenth century. The journal of Joseph Whitehouse, who accompanied Lewis and Clark on the expedition, provides evidence that cast iron Dutch ovens were carried on the journey. Another member of the expedition, John Coulter, held on to his cast iron Dutch oven until his dying days. After his death, it sold at auction for $4, the equivalent of a week's pay at the time.

The Dutch ovens that traveled west with the pioneers had legs enabling them to sit directly over a fire as well as hooks for hanging them above the flames. A flat, rimmed lid was designed to hold coals on top of the pot for even cooking. Today, Dutch ovens come in several varieties, including flat-bottomed pots with domed lids, made in both bare cast iron and cast iron coated with durable enamel, which are ideal for cooking on a stovetop. The traditional style of Dutch oven, though—with its three legs, bale handle for hanging, and flat, rimmed lid—is ideal for cooking over an open fire and is favored by campers to this day.

Why It's Great for Camping

From old-time pioneers to modern-day recreational campers, every outdoor adventurer knows that cooking good food in the great outdoors can be a challenge. A Dutch oven is a secret weapon that will help you emerge from your weekend in the woods victorious. While Dutch ovens, heavy as they are, aren't the kind of high-tech, ultra-light cooking gear you'd want to have with you on a backpacking trip, if you're car camping, or even able to drive to within a short walk to your campsite, these thick-walled, durable pots are by far the best way to make delicious food over a campfire.

SUPERIOR HEAT CONDUCTION

Dutch ovens, made of heavy-duty cast iron, get very, very hot. This very high heat helps caramelize the sugars in vegetables, fruits, and meats. This is key when cooking certain foods, like meat, which requires very high heat to form a crust that seals in its juices. Caramelization means deep, rich flavor in your finished dishes. Not only does cast iron get extremely hot, it also retains its heat. While pans made from other materials might drop in temperature the moment you add cold food, cast iron's temperature remains the same.

EVEN HEAT DISTRIBUTION

Dutch ovens are also wonders of heat distribution, heating so evenly that they are able to produce perfectly cooked stews, cornbread, and even cakes. Even heat distribution is key to cooking food consistently, no matter where it is in the pan.

VERSATILITY

A Dutch oven is perhaps the most versatile cooking pot around. Yes, it's fantastic for searing steaks, but you can also use it to simmer a pasta

Backyard Cooking

If you're anything like me, once you master Dutch oven camp cooking, you may not want to wait until your next camping trip for a spectacular campfire meal. You'll be glad to know that you can use your camp-style Dutch oven in any backyard fire pit or charcoal barbecue. You can use this setup to cook any of the recipes in this book, or try one of these surprising ways to make use of your Dutch oven without leaving home.

Enjoy a "Staycation" by Cooking Dutch Oven Meals in the Backyard. Kids, especially, will get a kick out of cooking dinner over a backyard fire pit. And, of course, using the fire afterwards to make s'mores for dessert is always a crowd pleaser. Plus, cleanup is easy.

Make Dutch Oven Lid Pizza. Who among us hasn't longed for a backyard pizza oven? Well, it turns out that a Dutch oven lid, turned upside down and heated over hot coals, makes a great pizza stone. It gets hot enough to help you mimic the effect of a fancy wood-burning oven.

Use Your Dutch Oven as a Smoker. It's easy to turn your Dutch oven into a backyard smoker. Just place a handful of food-smoking wood chips in the bottom of the pot, place a metal or wire trivet or grate over the wood chips, and then line the inside of the pot with foil. Poke several holes in the foil. Cover the pot with the lid and then preheat over hot coals (about ten to twelve coals for a 12-inch Dutch oven) for about fifteen minutes, until the wood begins to smoke. Add your food to the pot, replace the lid, and then place additional coals on top of the pot. Cooking time will vary depending on what you are cooking.

sauce, slow cook a meaty stew, roast vegetables, braise meat, gently sauté delicate foods, deep fry chicken to a crisp golden brown, or even bake a cake. And it can do all that over a campfire.

But that's not all it can do. You can use it as a mini grill for cooking skewers or kebabs. Just fill the Dutch oven with hot coals and lay your skewers across the top. Or use the lid—flipped upside down—as a griddle to cook everything from pancakes to pizza.

SAFE, ALL-NATURAL, NONSTICK SURFACE

Cast iron Dutch ovens, as long as they are well seasoned and well cared for, offer a nonstick surface without the use of any toxic chemicals that might break down in the high heat of a campfire and leach into your food. The nonstick quality of cast iron is also a bonus when it comes time to clean up. Who wants to spend their evening in the outdoors scrubbing dishes? With a good cast iron Dutch oven, cleanup requires only a minute or two with a bit of hot water and a sponge.

Finding the Right Fit

If you are looking to purchase your first camp Dutch oven, you'll quickly find that the variety can be overwhelming. Many different brands, sizes, shapes, materials, and price points are available, but there are a few key factors to consider.

Dishwashing at Camp

Cooking and eating great meals while camping has one negative side effect: dirty dishes. All of these recipes aim to dirty as few dishes as possible, but some dish washing is unavoidable. Here's what you'll need for an efficient dishwashing station:

- 2 tubs (I like to use collapsible buckets, which you can buy at any camping supply store)
- A pot or kettle for heating water
- A stove or fire to heat water
- Bleach
- Biodegradable dish soap
- 1 or 2 dish towels

Boil water on the stove or over the fire. Add some of the water to each of the tubs, then fill them the rest of the way with tap water. Add a capful of bleach to the first (washing) bucket to keep it clean and use a biodegradable dish soap to wash your dishes. Use the second bucket for rinsing. Lay a dish towel or two on a table near the buckets and stack the clean dishes there.

MATERIAL

Cast iron is the gold standard for Dutch ovens, and traditionalists recommend this type over modern options. Cast iron Dutch ovens are affordable, durable, and great for over-the-fire cooking. Their one drawback is their weight—an average-size cast iron Dutch oven can weigh as much as 20 pounds.

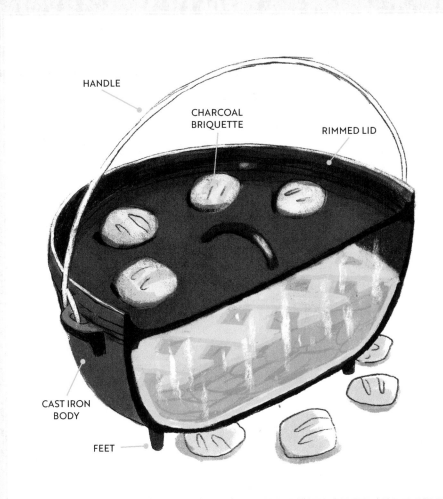

HANDLE

CHARCOAL
BRIQUETTE

RIMMED LID

CAST IRON
BODY

FEET

Some modern cookware producers make hard-anodized aluminum Dutch ovens, which are about two-thirds lighter than their iron counterparts, but still provide even heat distribution. These new-fangled Dutch ovens don't need to be seasoned either. The drawback? They cost about twice as much as the traditional cast iron type.

SIZE

Dutch ovens come in a wide range of sizes, starting with itty-bitty 1-quart pots and going up to 40 quarts or more. The recipes in this book have been created for cooking in a camp-style Dutch oven with a 12-inch diameter and a volume capacity of 6 quarts. This is a good starter-size pot that will allow you to comfortably cook meals for anywhere from 4 to 10 people.

LID TYPE

Dutch ovens intended for use on an indoor stovetop generally have domed lids. When purchasing a Dutch oven specifically for campfire cooking, look for one with a flat lid that has a rim or lip around the edge. This type of lid is designed to hold hot coals on the top, creating a true oven-like cooking environment with the heat source completely and evenly surrounding the pot. Check to be sure that the lid fits tightly and has a sturdy handle that is either a loop in the center of the lid or shaped like the handle of a skillet, extending out from the edge. The latter comes in handy when you want to flip the lid over and use it as a skillet or griddle.

BASE TYPE

As mentioned previously, camp-style Dutch ovens are designed specifically for cooking directly over hot coals. They have legs (usually 3) that elevate the pot a bit so that it can sit over the heat source. Choose a pot with sturdy, evenly spaced legs that are at least an inch tall so that the pot will be stable.

A good camp-style Dutch oven also has tabs on the sides for easy lifting and a sturdy wire bale handle that can be used either to lift the pot or suspend it from a cooking tripod.

Essential Equipment

A Dutch oven is a fantastically versatile cooking pot, which makes it a great addition to any camp kitchen. But while the Dutch oven may be the only pot you need to cook everything from breakfast to dessert, there are a few other essentials you'll want. There are also plenty of fancy, optional add-ons—cooking tripods, insulated storage bags, special Dutch oven tables, and the like—but you don't need any of these gadgets to use your Dutch oven in the great outdoors.

CHARCOAL

Some camp cooks like to cook over wood coals, but charcoal briquettes allow for much more control over the temperature of your fire. The recipes in this book are all designed for cooking with charcoal. Choose a natural-lighting charcoal and bring along a charcoal chimney starter (see below) so that you can avoid using lighter fluid, which is damaging to the environment.

CHARCOAL CHIMNEY STARTER

These are optional since many people prefer to use wood coals for cooking, but since the recipes in this book call for charcoal briquettes, having a charcoal chimney starter is very helpful. It is a metal cylinder with a grate inside. The briquettes go on top of the grate. A sheet of crumpled newspaper in the bottom is used to quickly and easily light charcoal and get it hot.

HEAVY-DUTY HEAT-RESISTANT GLOVES

The beauty of cast iron Dutch ovens is that they get really hot, but that means you need to be serious about protecting yourself from their heat. Look for gloves made of silicone, neoprene, or other heat-resistant materials that will cover your hands. It's also a good idea to invest in gloves that cover a good portion of your forearms for extra protection.

SHOVEL OR TONGS FOR ARRANGING HOT COALS

I like to use a sturdy pair of barbecue tongs to pick up hot coals (with my hand covered in a heat-resistant barbecue glove), to arrange the hot coals underneath the pot, and to lift them out of the fire pit and place them on top of the lid. A small shovel also works for this purpose, but I find the tongs easier to control.

LID LIFTER

Lid lifters are heavy-duty, long-handled hooks, usually made of steel, that allow you to lift the lid of your Dutch oven while keeping your hands and face at a safe distance from the pot and coals. These are a bit cumbersome but are handy when you've got a roiling pot of stew over a hot fire and it needs to be stirred. Look for one with a T-bar construction, which helps to stabilize the lid as you lift it.

LID STAND

A lid stand might seem like a superfluous accessory, but having a place to set the hot lid during cooking helps keep it clean. If you want to minimize your gear, however, you can fashion your own lid stand by creatively arranging a few rocks or sticks.

The Camper's Pantry

Having a well-stocked camp pantry will enable you to whip up delicious dishes with little effort. You don't need to bring your whole kitchen, but you'll be glad to have a handful of essentials along.

SPICES

Kosher salt and black pepper are the ultimate pantry essentials. Other herbs and spices are great for spicing up your meals. I always include a few basic dried herbs like oregano, rosemary, and basil as well as spices like cinnamon, cumin, cayenne, and chili powder. Other useful seasonings include garlic and onion powder, curry powder or paste, and ground mustard.

COOKING FATS

Cooking in a Dutch oven always requires some sort of cooking fat. Because Dutch oven cooking uses high heat, choose fats with high smoke points. These include cooking oils like peanut, coconut, sunflower seed, safflower, or avocado oil as well as animal fats like bacon fat, lard, or butter.

PRODUCE

Aromatics like onions, shallots, and garlic make a flavorful base for many dishes like stews, soups, and pasta sauces. They also store and travel

Adapting Recipes for Larger or Smaller Dutch Ovens

Dutch ovens come in all different shapes and sizes, but many Dutch oven recipes are easily adapted to fit the pot you have. Most soups, stews, and casserole-type dishes, for instance, are easily halved or doubled. Baked goods are trickier, however, since cooking times may change significantly based on volume.

The recipes in this book were adapted for a 12-inch, 6-quart Dutch oven. If yours is smaller or larger, you should have little trouble halving or doubling the recipes to fit, unless you are making baked goods (breads or cakes). Since the size of the pot and quantity of batter or dough can greatly effect baking times, I don't recommend trying to alter baked goods recipes unless you are up for experimenting until you get the result you desire.

well. Both the juice and zest of citrus fruits like lemons and limes are good for adding a burst of fresh flavor to many dishes.

CANNED GOODS

While the recipes in this book focus primarily on fresh ingredients, certain canned foods are really handy for outdoor cooking. Canned broths—chicken, beef, or vegetable—make flavorful bases for soups and stews. Canned diced tomatoes can be used in soups, stews, pasta sauces, and more. Canned beans can be added to chili, soups, or salads; turned into hearty vegetarian meals; or eaten hot as a healthy side dish.

CONDIMENTS

Condiments are instant flavor boosters, so they make great additions to a camp pantry. Vinegar (balsamic, wine, sherry, and others), soy sauce, mustard (Dijon, whole grain, honey, or whatever is your preference), ketchup, and hot sauce will keep your meals interesting.

SWEETENERS

With an assortment of condiments and spices, you've got savory dishes covered. Adding a sweetener or two allows you to whip up sweet treats, as well. Honey and maple syrup can be used to sweeten sauces or cakes, and they are also good for drizzling over pancakes, oatmeal, or fruit. White or brown sugar is great for baking and adding to your morning coffee.

How to Make a Camp Cooking Kit

When I first started camping, I used to stress out before every single trip making sure I had all the utensils, cookware, serving dishes, and dishwashing apparatus that I'd need. Eventually, I wised up and put together a movable camp kitchen. I keep everything in a lidded plastic tub in my garage so that I can be ready to hit the road on a moment's notice, confident that I have all of the essentials.

You can buy everything you need either at camping supply stores or places like Target or Walmart, but I put together most of my original camp cooking kit at local thrift stores. As a result, I saved money and loaded up on sturdy items that I wasn't attached to. Over the years, I've replaced many items with newer, lighter-weight, or more durable items.

Here's what you need for a minimal but well-equipped camp kitchen:

- Your trusty Dutch oven and accessories (page 10)
- Plates and mugs (bowls are nice to have, but you can eat soup or stew out of mugs if needed)
- Forks, spoons, knives
- Bottle opener/corkscrew
- Can opener
- Cutting board (I like a durable plastic cutting board that can be sanitized in the dishwasher once I return home)
- Sharp knife for chopping vegetables and fruit, slicing meat, etc.
- Long-handled tongs, for both cooking and serving
- Long-handled serving utensils including a spoon, spatula, and ladle
- Kettle (for boiling water)
- Sponge
- Two tubs for washing and rinsing dishes (look for collapsible tubs to save space)
- Biodegradable dish soap (available at camping supply stores)
- Dish towels

Chapter Two

Getting Started

ONCE YOU'VE ACQUIRED YOUR CAMP-STYLE DUTCH OVEN and accessories, assembled a camp cooking kit, and stocked your camp pantry, it's time to get started using your Dutch oven to cook some of the best meals of your life—whether in your backyard at home or out in the wilderness.

How to Season Cast Iron

Seasoning is a simple process that gives your cast iron cookware a non-stick coating, making it both easy to cook in and easy to clean. The clean, dry cast iron surface is coated with a thin layer of oil and then heated to a high temperature. This causes a chemical reaction between the metal and the fat in which the surface becomes polymerized. In other words, the fat bonds with the metal to create an extremely durable, nonstick, plastic-like coating. If you purchase a new cast iron pan, the box will likely proclaim that it is "preseasoned," suggesting that you can cook with it right away. Regardless, I strongly recommend that you reseason it if you have the time. A good, thick layer of seasoning takes several applications to build.

New or old, any Dutch oven should be scrubbed before seasoning. Coarse kosher salt makes a great scouring powder that won't damage your pan. Use a hefty amount of kosher salt and a paper towel to scrub off any dust, residue, or rust spots. Wash the pan well with hot water and a mild soap if you wish (I'll address the soap vs. no soap issue in the next section) and then dry it thoroughly. Follow the steps below for seasoning your Dutch oven either at home or at a campsite.

SEASONING YOUR DUTCH OVEN IN YOUR HOME KITCHEN

1. Preheat both the Dutch oven and lid by placing them in a preheated 200°F oven for 15 minutes. This opens up its pores so it is more receptive to the oil.

2. Oil both the Dutch oven and lid inside and out. You can use just about any type of cooking oil to season cast iron cookware, but the best choices are neutral-flavored oils with high smoke points like corn, vegetable, safflower, or flaxseed. Use a paper towel soaked in oil to coat every surface of the Dutch oven and wipe off excess. You want a very thin layer that completely coats the metal surface.

3. Heat the oven to at least 400°F (up to 500°F if your oven goes that high). Place the Dutch oven and lid on the center rack in the oven upside down (to allow excess oil to drip off as it heats instead of pooling in the center) and place a baking sheet or piece of aluminum foil below them to catch any dripping oil. Heat for 1 hour.

4. Turn off the oven's heat, but leave the Dutch oven and lid inside to cool for 2 to 3 hours.

5. Repeat steps 2, 3, and 4 several times, until your Dutch oven and lid have a deep, black, glossy sheen.

SEASONING YOUR DUTCH OVEN AT YOUR CAMPSITE

1. Using a hardwood like hickory or oak, build a very hot fire in either a fire pit or barbecue.

2. Place a grill or grate over the fire. Place the Dutch oven and lid on the grate and heat for about 15 minutes.

3. Oil both the Dutch oven and lid inside and out. You can use just about any type of cooking oil to season cast iron cookware, but the best choices are neutral-flavored oils with high smoke points like corn, vegetable, safflower, or flaxseed. Use a paper towel soaked in oil to coat every surface of the Dutch oven and wipe off the excess. You want a very thin layer that completely coats the metal surface.

4. Place the Dutch oven and lid upside down on the grate. Let the fire do its work until it dies out naturally. Leave the Dutch oven and lid on the grate until it is cool enough to pick up with your bare hands.

5. Repeat steps 1 through 4 as needed to achieve a deep, glossy sheen.

Cast Iron Care

Cast iron holds the peculiar distinction of being one of the most beloved, and, at the same time, one of the most anxiety-inducing types of cookware. Cooks love it for its all-natural nonstick coating, its durability and

Safety

A book dealing with cooking with hot coals would not be complete without an overview on safety. Many of the potential hazards of camp cooking are no different than those present in your home kitchen, but cooking outdoors or at a campsite presents certain unique dangers.

1. When building a fire outdoors, keep a bucket of water nearby in case of an unexpected flare-up.

2. Always use a designated fire pit or barbecue if there is one at the campsite.

3. If there is no designated fire pit or barbecue, check the campground or park regulations to make sure that fires are allowed. If so, build your fire in a well-ventilated area that is clear of wooden structures, trees, dry leaves, and other flammable materials. Build your fire in an area covered with bare earth or rock.

4. Always wear protective hand coverings when cooking in cast iron as the metal gets extremely hot. Use a lid lifter and lid stand as needed to maneuver the hot parts of your Dutch oven during cooking and serving.

5. Never leave a fire unattended.

6. Bury your fire in ashes when you are finished cooking and from a safe distance monitor the area until the coals are completely cooled.

versatility, and its superior heat-conduction capabilities. And yet, even the most competent cooks are anxious when it comes to the care and maintenance of cast iron, so much so that many avoid using this type of cookware altogether. Rest assured, this fear is uncalled for. Cleaning and maintaining your cast iron is easier than you think.

CLEANING

To keep your cast iron Dutch oven in prime condition, be sure to clean it immediately after use. Here are 4 ways to clean your cast iron cookware:

Hot water and a (non-metal) scrubber. This is by far the simplest and most common cleaning method. If your skillet is well-seasoned, food particles should come right off with just a bit of gentle scrubbing, some hot water, and a sponge or a stiff, natural or plastic (not wire), bristle brush.

Boiling water. If you're having trouble removing stuck-on food, rinse the skillet while it is still hot. Fill the skillet again with water and bring to a boil over the fire. Boil for a few minutes to break up stuck-on food. Use a spatula if needed to dislodge food residue, lightly scraping the bottom and sides of the pan. Be careful to do this gently so that you don't scrape off the pan's seasoning layers.

Kosher salt. If you are still left with lots of stuck-on food residue, make a paste of coarse kosher salt and warm water, and use it as a scrub to scour off stuck-on food.

Hot soapy water. I'm sure you've heard that you should never use soap on your cast iron cookware, but it turns out that this warning is unfounded. Yes, harsh dish soaps are designed to cut through oil, and since seasoning is done with oil, it seems logical that soap would take off your precious seasoning. But in reality, your seasoning is a layer of polymerized oil. This means that the oil has undergone a chemical reaction that has turned it into a plastic-like coating that is bonded to the metal. A dishwashing liquid designed for hand washing won't be able to strip that away. So, go ahead and lather up if you like. Be sure to avoid harsh soaps.

When you have finished cleaning and drying your Dutch oven, heat it briefly over a medium fire and then rub a lightly oil-soaked paper towel over the interior of the pot. Wipe again with a clean paper towel to remove any excess oil. Allow the pan to cool before storing.

STORING AND TRANSPORTING

Always clean your Dutch oven thoroughly and dry it completely before storing it. Place a paper towel, dish towel, or a sheet of newspaper inside of it to absorb any moisture. Store the pot with the lid on, but place a folded paper towel under the lid to allow air to circulate, which will prevent the seasoning layer from becoming rancid.

You can purchase a specially designed fabric bag designed for storing and transporting a Dutch oven, or simply use a large paper bag, a cardboard box, or an old pillowcase.

RESEASONING

After repeated use, you may notice that food has begun to stick to the surface of your Dutch oven, the finish has become dull, or visible rust has developed. These are all signs that it is time to reseason. To do so, scrub the pot extremely well with hot, soapy water and a stiff (non-metal) brush or scrubber. In this case, it is okay to use harsher, grease-cutting detergents since your goal is to take the pot back to its preseasoned state. Rinse the pot and dry it well.

If rust has formed, submerge the pot in a solution made of one part distilled vinegar and one part cold water. After a few minutes, the rust should begin to bubble off. Rinse and dry the skillet thoroughly.

Now that you have brought your Dutch oven back to its original, unseasoned state, immediately revisit the seasoning steps outlined on page 20. As before, repeat the process several times to re-create a deep, black, glossy sheen.

Camp Cooking

Now that your Dutch oven is seasoned, it's time to get cooking. The recipes in this book are all designed to be cooked using charcoal briquettes in a fire pit or barbecue. Follow these step-by-step directions and prepare to dazzle your companions with delicious meals.

Cast Iron Care—Always and Never

ALWAYS

- Season new cast iron cookware thoroughly by going through the seasoning process several times before using it to cook.
- Clean immediately after use.
- Dry immediately after washing.
- Rub your Dutch oven with a bit of cooking oil immediately after cleaning and drying it.
- Reseason your Dutch oven whenever its surface becomes dull or rusty or food begins to stick to it.

NEVER

- Leave a hot Dutch oven unattended where an unsuspecting person might touch it.
- Use a harsh abrasive like steel wool to scrub your Dutch oven.
- Leave your Dutch oven soaking in water for any length of time.
- Leave your Dutch oven wet after washing.
- Let food sit in your Dutch oven for long periods or use the Dutch oven to store leftover food.

PREP THE COALS

Light about 30 to 40 briquettes. If using a chimney starter, put the briquettes in the chimney on top of the grate and put the chimney starter on top of the grill or in the fire pit. Place a sheet or two of crumpled newspaper underneath the grate in the chimney and light it on fire. Let burn for about 10 to 15 minutes, until the briquettes begin to glow red and flames come out of the top of the chimney. Pour the coals out into a pile in the middle of the fire pit or barbecue. Once the coals are completely or mostly covered in gray ash (after an additional 5 or 10 minutes), they are ready for cooking and can be spread out into an even layer.

ARRANGE THE COALS

A general rule of thumb for Dutch oven cooking with charcoal is to double the diameter of the Dutch oven to determine how many coals to use to create a moderate-heat cooking environment (around 350°F). Using this formula, a 12-inch Dutch oven would require 24 coals, while a 14-inch Dutch oven would require 28. Whether you put the coals underneath or on top of the oven—or both—depends on what type of cooking you are doing. For higher-heat cooking, such as for roasting or deep-frying, add more coals (two additional coals will add about 50°F to the temperature.)

Coals should be arranged underneath the oven in a circular pattern, spacing them about an inch apart and leaving the very center of the circle empty to avoid creating a hot spot in the center of the oven that could burn your food. The evenly spaced, circular arrangement of the coals serves to distribute the heat evenly under the pot.

Similarly, coals placed on top of the lid should be evenly spaced, about an inch apart, in a circular pattern around the outer edge of the lid with a few coals placed in the center near the handle.

The guidelines below assume that you are using a 12-inch diameter Dutch oven. For a larger or smaller oven, adjust the number of coals accordingly.

Method 1: Stovetop Cooking

For boiling water, simmering soups and sauces, making stews and chilies, sautéing, boiling, stir-frying, or deep-frying, all of the coals should be arranged underneath the Dutch oven in order to mimic the effect of cooking on a stovetop. This means that for your 12-inch Dutch oven, you would arrange 24 coals underneath.

Method 2: Baking

To create a medium-heat, oven-like cooking environment (about 350°F), place about 8 of the coals underneath the pot and 16 on top. This is the ideal temperature for making baked pasta dishes, meatloaves, and cakes.

Method 3: Roasting

Roasting is similar to baking but requires higher heat. To increase the heat to about 450°F, use the setup for baking (8 coals underneath, 16 on top), but add two additional coals to both the top and bottom. The higher heat is perfect for roasting vegetables and meats.

Method 4: Broiling

You can turn your Dutch oven into a broiler by arranging all the coals on the top of the oven. This method allows you to create crispy toppings for casseroles and baked goods.

Oven Temperature Conversion Chart

This chart outlines oven temperature conversions for camp-style Dutch ovens.

Oven Temperature	Number of Coals		
	10-INCH DUTCH OVEN	12-INCH DUTCH OVEN	14-INCH DUTCH OVEN
300 degrees	7 on Top 11 on Bottom	9 on Top 13 on Bottom	11 on Top 15 on Bottom
350 degrees	8 on Top 12 on Bottom	8 on Top 16 on Bottom	12 on Top 16 on Bottom
400 degrees	9 on Top 13 on Bottom	9 on Top 17 on Bottom	13 on Top 17 on Bottom
450 degrees	10 on Top 14 on Bottom	10 on Top 18 on Bottom	14 on Top 18 on Bottom
500 degrees	11 on Top 15 on Bottom	11 on Top 19 on Bottom	15 on Top 19 on Bottom

The Campfire Method

Some traditionalists prefer to cook over embers created by burning hardwood rather than charcoal. Although it is more challenging to control, the heat these embers put out is higher than what you can get from charcoal. To cook using wood embers, follow these steps.

1. Using several logs of hardwood, like hickory or mesquite, build a fire off to one side in a fire pit. If there isn't one available, create one with a ring of rocks in a clear area away from flammable materials. Let the fire burn until the flames are nearly out and the embers are glowing red.

2. Create a cooking hearth by clearing an area in the fire pit near the fire. If you don't have sufficient legs on your Dutch oven, use four softball-size rocks to create an elevated cooking platform with space in the center for hot coals.

3. Using a small shovel, long-handled tongs, or a stick, move some of the hot embers to your hearth and place the Dutch oven on top. Add embers to the top of the pot using a shovel or tongs. Just like in cooking with charcoal, you can control the heat by using more or fewer embers both on top of and beneath the pot.

Meal Planning

Meal planning is an essential part of camp cooking. And good planning is key to any successful camping trip. The following tips will help you create a stress-free meal plan that will make campsite mealtimes both fun and satisfying.

CREATE A DAY-BY-DAY, MEAL-BY-MEAL PLAN

Once you've nailed down the basic details of your trip, create a meal plan that covers each meal that you'll cook while away. Include plans for breakfast, lunch, dinner, and snacks each day. Once the plan is complete, create a detailed shopping list covering all of the ingredients, condiments, sides, and other items needed for all of the meals.

KEEP PERISHABILITY IN MIND AS YOU PLAN

When planning your menu, keep in mind how long different foods will last in a cooler, and plan to cook the most perishable foods early on in the trip. Fish, for instance, shouldn't be kept for more than a day or two, while steak (properly stored) will be fine for up to five days. Likewise, lettuce begins to wilt after a day or two, but heartier vegetables—such as asparagus, cauliflower, and zucchini—can last up to a week. Cheese, tofu, and precooked meats, such as smoked sausages, will last a week or longer in a cooler. Canned beans are a great failsafe protein to have along for the final meals of a long trip.

KEEP IT SIMPLE

Keep your meal planning simple by using some of the same ingredients in more than one meal. For instance, you might use salsa and sour cream as condiments on breakfast burritos and then again later for Salsa Verde Chilaquiles (page 61), or as a snack with a bag of tortilla chips.

SHARE THE LOAD

If you are traveling with other adults, you might want to divide the meals up among people (or groups of people) so that no one person has to do all of the work. Have each person, couple, or group plan an equal number of meals. This keeps meal planning fun rather than having it become a heavy burden for the one cook in the group.

Sample Menus

The following are three sample camping meal plans that cover meals from Friday lunch through Sunday breakfast (2 lunches, 2 dinners, 2 breakfasts) as well as snacks and treats.

MEMORIAL DAY

	FRIDAY	SATURDAY	SUNDAY
BREAKFAST	*Set up Camp*	Potato, egg, and cheese scramble made with leftover potatoes	Salsa Verde Chilaquiles (with salsa and sour cream garnish) (page 61)
LUNCH	Cold cuts and cheese sandwiches (including sandwich bread, mustard, mayonnaise, pickles, tomatoes, and lettuce) Fresh fruit Carrot sticks	Chicken salad sandwiches with leftover Balsamic-Braised Chicken (sandwich bread, mayo, spices, tomato, and lettuce) Fresh fruit Celery sticks	*Head Home!*
SNACK	Chips and salsa	Leftover Pineapple Upside-Down Cake	
DINNER	Balsamic-Braised Chicken (page 96) Grilled asparagus Foil-wrapped fire-baked potatoes	Fish Stew with Tomatoes (page 70) Crusty No-Knead French Bread (page 148) Salad (lettuce, cucumber, radishes, and dressing)	
DESSERT	Pineapple Upside-Down Cake (page 162)	Double-Chocolate Brownies (page 165)	

8 Camping Hacks

Living outdoors, even for just a few days, creates a few challenges. Make your camping life easier by using these simple hacks for a fun, stress-free trip.

1. Make campsite cooking easier by premeasuring dry ingredients and putting them in a clearly labeled resealable plastic bag.

2. Pre-marinate meats at home, packing them into labeled resealable plastic bags. You'll enhance the flavor by marinating the meat for longer, plus you won't have to bring all the individual ingredients for the marinade.

3. Freeze foods like meats (in marinade if possible), fish, or hearty vegetables. They will last longer and help keep the food in your cooler cold.

4. Pre-chop vegetables at home, especially things like onions and garlic that you'll use in multiple recipes. Just be sure to bring enough for all of the recipes.

5. Bring along headlamps. These make great hands-free flashlights that will help you get around your campsite in the dark. They also make tasks like cooking or washing dishes in the dark much easier. Plus, you can strap them to a water jug (with the light facing into the jug) for an instant lantern!

6. Eliminate the need for a pillow by stuffing clean clothes into your sleeping bag's stuff sack for a soft place to rest your head.

7. Dryer lint makes a nifty fire starter. Instead of tossing it in the trash, put it in a bag. When the bag is full, tuck it into your camping gearbox for your next trip.

8. Invest in a few microfiber towels. They are lightweight, highly absorbent, and dry quickly.

4TH OF JULY

	FRIDAY	SATURDAY	SUNDAY
BREAKFAST	*Set up Camp*	Cinnamon-Raisin Breakfast Bread Pudding (page 43)	Blueberry Breakfast Cake (page 46)
LUNCH	Hot dogs and fixings (buns, relish, mustard, and ketchup) Potato chips Fresh fruit	Cheeseburgers (buns, mustard, relish, ketchup, tomato, onion, and lettuce) Cucumber salad Fresh fruit	*Head Home!*
SNACK	Guacamole and chips	Trail mix	
DINNER	One-Pot Spaghetti in Meat Sauce (page 108) Rosemary Olive Oil Bread (page 152) Salad (lettuce, tomatoes, cucumbers, and dressing)	Cider and Dijon Roast Pork (page 111) Rice pilaf Grilled Brussels sprouts on skewers	
DESSERT	Brown Sugar Berry Crisp (page 156)	Dutch Oven Layered Banana S'mores Pie (page 166)	

LABOR DAY

	FRIDAY	SATURDAY	SUNDAY
BREAKFAST	*Set up Camp*	Strawberry Dutch Baby (page 44)	Savory Sausage and Cheese French Toast Casserole (page 56)
LUNCH	Crispy Beer-Battered Fried Fish (with tartar sauce) (page 95) Salad (lettuce, tomato, cucumber, and dressing)	Spicy Beef and Bean Chili (with salsa, sour cream, and cheese) (page 74) Honey-Sweetened Cornbread (page 143) Fresh fruit	*Head Home!*
SNACK	Cheesy Biscuits (page 138)	Chips and salsa	
DINNER	Classic Meatloaf (page 117) Creamy Mashed Potatoes with Greek Yogurt (page 128) Sautéed green beans	Whole Roast Chicken with Root Vegetables (page 99) Grilled zucchini	
DESSERT	Gooey Caramel Baked Apples (page 157)	Sunny Orange Cake (page 161)	

About the Recipes

The recipes in this book were developed to step up your camp-cooking game effortlessly. They are inspired and creative, but they do not require long lists of ingredients, hard-to-find ingredients, or unhealthy processed foods. In fact, they use fresh ingredients whenever possible and are intended to be both nutritious and satisfying.

5 INGREDIENTS OR LESS

Every recipe in this book requires five ingredients or less, not counting basics like cooking oil, salt, pepper, garlic, and sugar.

LABELS

Since camping groups often include people with various dietary restrictions and food allergies as well as a few plain picky eaters, I've included recipes to address many different dietary concerns. These include recipes that are Vegan, Vegetarian, Gluten-Free, Nut-Free, and Soy-Free. You'll find these labels at the top of the recipes for easy reference.

Note:
The recipes can all be adapted for a stovetop Dutch oven as well—just use the temperature chart on page 31 to determine the required oven temperature.

Chapter Three

Breakfast

ALL-PURPOSE BAKING MIX

VEGETARIAN
SOY-FREE
NUT-FREE

MAKES 4½ CUPS

PREP TIME
5 MINUTES

COOK TIME
NONE

Camp Hack:

Mix a batch of this and then store it in pre-measured portions in resealable plastic bags with the recipe it is intended for printed on the bag.

Variation:

For pancakes, follow the directions for biscuit dough, but add additional milk to thin it out to pancake batter consistency.

This is a base recipe for a dry mix that you can make at home and use at your campsite to make pancakes, biscuits, scones, cakes, and more. To make basic biscuit dough, combine 2 cups all-purpose baking mix with ½ cup butter, vegetable shortening, or coconut oil, and ½ cup milk.

4 CUPS ALL-PURPOSE FLOUR
½ CUP DRIED MILK POWDER
2 TABLESPOONS BAKING POWDER
1 TEASPOON BAKING SODA
1 TEASPOON KOSHER SALT

Mix all of the ingredients together and store in a sealable container or resealable plastic bag for up to 3 months.

CINNAMON-RAISIN BREAKFAST BREAD PUDDING

VEGETARIAN
SOY-FREE
NUT-FREE

SERVES 6 TO 8

PREP TIME
10 MINUTES

COOK TIME
45 MINUTES

24 COALS

Make Ahead:

If you want to get a head start on breakfast, you can mix up the milk, eggs, sugar, vanilla, and bread in a large, resealable plastic bag (or two) the night before and store it in your cooler overnight. Note: You might want to double bag it to prevent leakage.

Waking up at a campsite usually means reluctantly extricating yourself from a warm sleeping bag in order to get a fire—and breakfast—going. Once you're enjoying this warm, sweet, spiced pudding, you'll be a happy camper for sure. Using cinnamon-raisin bread is a clever way to cut down on the number of ingredients you need to bring along.

¼ CUP (½ STICK) UNSALTED BUTTER

4 CUPS WHOLE MILK

8 LARGE EGGS

¼ CUP BROWN SUGAR

2 TEASPOONS VANILLA EXTRACT

1 (1-POUND) LOAF CINNAMON-RAISIN BREAD, CUT INTO CUBES

1   Melt the butter in the Dutch oven over a bed of 10 hot coals. Remove the pot from the heat and add the milk, eggs, brown sugar, and vanilla extract. Whisk to combine well. Stir in the cubed bread until well coated. Cover the Dutch oven and return it to the bed of hot coals. Place 14 hot coals on the lid.

2   Bake for about 45 minutes, until the mixture has set and is springy to the touch. Serve hot, sprinkled with brown sugar or maple syrup, if desired.

STRAWBERRY DUTCH BABY

VEGETARIAN
SOY-FREE
NUT-FREE

SERVES 6

PREP TIME
5 MINUTES

COOK TIME
25 MINUTES

28 COALS

Seasonal Swap:
You can use any type of berries or stone fruits like nectarines or peaches when strawberries are out of season.

A Dutch baby (also called a German pancake) is a large, puffy pancake that is often served with fruit or dusted with powdered sugar and a drizzle of lemon juice. It can be topped with any number of fruits or other sweet toppings. This version uses juicy strawberries that have been macerated in a bit of sugar.

3 LARGE EGGS

⅔ CUP ALL-PURPOSE FLOUR

⅔ CUP MILK

⅛ TEASPOON SALT

¼ CUP (½ STICK) UNSALTED BUTTER, CUT INTO PIECES

1 PINT STRAWBERRIES, HALVED OR QUARTERED IF LARGE

⅓ CUP SUGAR

1 In a large bowl, whisk the eggs until they are frothy and pale yellow. Add the flour, milk, and salt and whisk until smooth.

2 Melt the butter in the Dutch oven set over 12 hot coals. Add the batter, cover the pot, and place 16 hot coals on the lid.

3 Bake for about 20 minutes, checking that the batter puffs up and turns golden brown.

4 While the pancake is baking, combine the strawberries and sugar in a medium bowl and stir to coat.

5 Pour the strawberry mixture, along with the accumulated juices, over the middle of the Dutch Baby. Cut into wedges and serve immediately.

LEMON BUTTERMILK BISCUITS

VEGETARIAN
SOY-FREE
NUT-FREE

MAKES 16 BISCUITS

PREP TIME
10 MINUTES

COOK TIME
15 MINUTES

26 COALS

Variation:
Add ½ cup of your favorite dried fruits like raisins or chopped apricots to the dough before cooking.

Instead of actual buttermilk, these biscuits use regular milk that's been "acidified" with lemon juice. Along with the lemon zest, this adds bright flavor and gives the biscuits the flakiness you'd expect from buttermilk dough.

½ CUP MILK

2 TEASPOONS FRESHLY SQUEEZED LEMON JUICE, PLUS ZEST FROM 1 LEMON

2 CUPS ALL-PURPOSE BAKING MIX (PAGE 42), OR STORE-BOUGHT BISCUIT MIX

3 TABLESPOONS SUGAR

½ CUP (1 STICK) UNSALTED BUTTER, MELTED, PLUS ADDITIONAL FOR PREPARING THE DUTCH OVEN

1 LARGE EGG, BEATEN

1 In a small bowl or cup, combine the milk and lemon juice and let stand for 5 to 10 minutes.

2 In a large bowl, mix the milk and lemon juice mixture with the lemon zest, baking mix, sugar, butter, and egg using your hands, until it forms into a soft sticky dough.

3 Form the dough into golf ball–size balls and then flatten each into a patty about ½ inch thick and 2½ inches wide.

4 Coat the Dutch oven lightly with butter and place it over a bed of 10 hot coals. Let the pot heat up for about 5 minutes, then add the dough patties in a single layer. Cover the pot and place 16 hot coals on the lid. Cook for about 5 minutes, then carefully remove the lid with a lid lifter keeping the coals in place, flip the biscuits, replace the lid with the coals on top, and cook for another 5 minutes, or until the biscuits are golden brown and cooked through. Serve hot.

BLUEBERRY BREAKFAST CAKE

VEGETARIAN
SOY-FREE
NUT-FREE

SERVES 8

PREP TIME
10 MINUTES

COOK TIME
50 MINUTES

24 COALS

Variation:
For a special touch,
add a sweet glaze to
the top of the cake.
Stir together 1 cup
powdered sugar with
2 tablespoons water
until smooth. Drizzle
the glaze over the
cooled cake before
serving.

I don't know about you, but I think camping is a perfect excuse to eat cake for breakfast. Besides, you won't feel so bad about this one because it is made with Greek yogurt and blueberries, so it's practically health food. Serve this cake dolloped with additional vanilla yogurt and topped with fresh fruit, if you like.

½ CUP COOKING OIL, PLUS ADDITIONAL FOR
   PREPARING THE DUTCH OVEN

4 LARGE EGGS

¾ CUP SUGAR

1 CUP VANILLA GREEK YOGURT

2 CUPS ALL-PURPOSE BAKING MIX (PAGE 42),
   OR STORE-BOUGHT BISCUIT MIX

1 CUP FRESH OR FROZEN BLUEBERRIES

1   Coat the Dutch oven lightly with cooking oil.

2   In a large bowl, whisk together the eggs, sugar, and Greek yogurt. Add the baking mix and whisk to incorporate. Stir in the oil until it is completely incorporated. Gently fold in the blueberries.

3   Pour the batter into the Dutch oven and place the Dutch oven over a bed of 10 hot coals. Place the lid on the Dutch oven and top with 14 hot coals. Bake for about 50 minutes, until the cake is springy to the touch and a toothpick inserted into the center comes out clean. Remove the Dutch oven from the heat, remove the lid, and let the cake cool for about 10 minutes.

4   To serve, loosen the cake from the sides of the Dutch oven by running a knife around the outer edge of the cake. Invert onto a platter, if desired, cut into wedges, and serve.

APPLE COFFEE CAKE

VEGETARIAN
SOY-FREE
NUT-FREE

SERVES 8

PREP TIME
10 MINUTES

COOK TIME
40 MINUTES

24 COALS

Variation:
Spice this recipe up by adding ½ teaspoon of ground cinnamon to the batter or to the topping mixture.

Make Ahead:
If you are planning on making this dish the first morning, prepare the apple the day before and store in your cooler in a resealable bag.

There is no better accompaniment to a hot cup of coffee than a slice of warm, sweet, streusel-topped coffee cake. Enjoy this winning combination while warming yourself near a hot fire on a cool, crisp morning in the outdoors.

¼ CUP UNSALTED BUTTER, CUT INTO SMALL
PIECES, PLUS ADDITIONAL FOR PREPARING
THE DUTCH OVEN

2 CUPS PLUS ⅓ CUP ALL-PURPOSE BAKING
MIX (PAGE 42), DIVIDED

⅔ CUP WATER

⅓ CUP PLUS 2 TABLESPOONS BROWN
SUGAR, DIVIDED

1 LARGE EGG

1 GREEN APPLE, PEELED, CORED, AND DICED

1 Coat the Dutch oven lightly with butter.

2 In the Dutch oven, mix together 2 cups baking mix, ⅔ cup water, 2 tablespoons brown sugar, egg, and apple. Smooth the top into an even layer.

3 In a medium bowl, combine the remaining ⅓ cup baking mix, the remaining ⅓ cup brown sugar, and the remaining ¼ cup butter, rubbing the mixture between your hands until it resembles a coarse meal. Sprinkle the mixture evenly over the cake batter in the Dutch oven.

4 Place the Dutch oven over a bed of 10 hot coals. Cover the pot and place 14 hot coals on the lid. Bake for about 40 minutes, until a toothpick inserted into the center comes out clean. Remove the lid from the pot, remove the pot from the heat, and let cool for at least 15 minutes. Cut the cake into wedges and serve.

SWIRLED CINNAMON CAKE

VEGETARIAN
SOY-FREE
NUT-FREE

SERVES 8

PREP TIME
10 MINUTES

COOK TIME
40 MINUTES

24 COALS

Variation:

Serve wedges of this cake topped with yogurt and fresh fruit—blueberries, peaches, pears, or even a combination of fruits—for a filling breakfast.

This is one of my favorite camping breakfasts: a fluffy cinnamon cake with rivers of sweet cinnamon-sugar filling swirled throughout. It delivers the wonderful flavors of cinnamon buns, but with less work.

3 CUPS PLUS 2 TABLESPOONS ALL-PURPOSE BAKING MIX (PAGE 42), OR STORE-BOUGHT BAKING MIX

2 CUPS BROWN SUGAR, DIVIDED

1½ CUPS WATER

2 LARGE EGGS

1 CUP (2 STICKS) UNSALTED BUTTER, AT ROOM TEMPERATURE, DIVIDED

2 TABLESPOONS CINNAMON

1 In a large bowl, stir together 3 cups All-Purpose Baking Mix, 1 cup brown sugar, the water, and eggs until smooth and well combined.

2 Melt ½ cup of the butter in the Dutch oven set over a bed of 10 hot coals. Remove the pot from the coals and stir in the cake batter mixture, mixing until the butter is incorporated. Smooth the batter out into an even layer.

3 In a medium bowl, mash together the remaining ½ cup of butter, the remaining cup of brown sugar, the remaining 2 tablespoons All-Purpose Baking Mix, and the cinnamon. Drop this mixture by spoonfuls onto the cake batter. Use a knife or spoon to swirl the butter-cinnamon mixture into the batter.

4 Return the Dutch oven to the bed of 10 hot coals. Cover the pot and place 14 hot coals on the lid. Bake for about 40 minutes, until a toothpick inserted into the center comes out clean. Remove the cake from the oven and let cool for a few minutes. Slice into wedges and serve.

BROWN SUGAR–BAKED OATMEAL

VEGETARIAN
GLUTEN-FREE
SOY-FREE
NUT-FREE

SERVES 8

PREP TIME
5 MINUTES

COOK TIME
30 MINUTES

26 COALS

This simple, lightly sweetened baked oatmeal is a great way to serve a healthy breakfast to a crowd. Serve it as is and let people add whatever toppings they like—chopped fresh fruit, peanut butter, maple syrup, raisins, ground cinnamon, or more brown sugar for example—or add a cup or two of sliced bananas, chopped apples, diced peaches, or other fruit to the mix before baking.

COOKING OIL FOR PREPARING THE
   DUTCH OVEN
4 CUPS OLD-FASHIONED ROLLED OATS
   (GLUTEN-FREE, IF NECESSARY)
½ CUP BROWN SUGAR
2 TEASPOONS BAKING POWDER
½ TEASPOON KOSHER SALT
2 LARGE EGGS, LIGHTLY BEATEN
3 CUPS MILK

1 Coat the Dutch oven lightly with cooking oil.

2 In the Dutch oven, stir together the oats, brown sugar, baking powder, and salt. Stir in the eggs and milk.

3 Cover the pot and place the Dutch oven over a bed of 11 hot coals. Place 15 hot coals on the lid. Bake for about 30 minutes, until the mixture is firm and cooked through. Cut into wedges and serve warm.

Camp Hack:

Mix up the dry ingredients (oats, brown sugar, baking powder, and salt) before you leave home, storing them in a resealable plastic bag. Write the cooking instructions right on the bag so you'll know exactly what to add and how to cook it at camp.

Essential Technique:

Baked oatmeal is a great base recipe that is easily changed up for variety. Add nuts or fruit before baking, or create a breakfast bar of toppings—yogurt, fresh fruit, dried fruit, nuts and seeds, shredded coconut, or other toppings—and let everyone participate by creating their own ideal breakfast bowl.

STRAWBERRY STEEL-CUT OATS

VEGAN
GLUTEN-FREE
SOY-FREE
NUT-FREE

SERVES 6

PREP TIME
5 MINUTES

COOK TIME
25 MINUTES

14 COALS

Variation:
Use any type of jam, jelly, or preserves to suit your taste. Add a sprinkling of chopped walnuts or almonds for added protein.

This quick-to-make hot cereal breakfast is sweetened with a combination of strawberry preserves and brown sugar (you can substitute maple syrup for the brown sugar, if you like), giving it a lovely pink hue and a bright, fruity flavor.

1½ CUPS STEEL-CUT OATS
5 CUPS WATER
¼ CUP STRAWBERRY PRESERVES
PINCH OF KOSHER SALT
3 TABLESPOONS BROWN SUGAR

1 Place the Dutch oven over a bed of 14 hot coals. Add the oats and toast, stirring occasionally, until they begin to turn golden and smell nutty, about 3 minutes. Stir in the water, preserves, and salt. Bring to a boil and then remove 4 to 6 of the coals underneath the pot, reducing the heat to a simmer.

2 Cook, stirring occasionally and adding additional water if necessary, until the oats are tender, about 20 minutes. Serve hot, sprinkled with additional brown sugar or a bit of maple syrup, if desired.

HONEY-ALMOND GRANOLA BARS

VEGETARIAN
GLUTEN-FREE
SOY-FREE

MAKES ABOUT
12 BARS

PREP TIME
10 MINUTES

COOK TIME
5 MINUTES

10 COALS

Variation:
Dress these up by adding up to a cup of chopped dried fruit, shredded coconut, a combination of different nuts, or even chocolate chips. Stir these additions into the mixture along with the oats and almonds.

Honey-almond granola bars are easy to make in a Dutch oven, and they make a filling breakfast. You can make them in the morning or make them ahead of time to eliminate any morning work. They pair perfectly with a hot cup of coffee and are also easy to tuck into a backpack for a hearty trailside snack later during your trip.

COOKING OIL FOR PREPARING THE
  DUTCH OVEN

2½ CUPS OLD-FASHIONED ROLLED OATS
  (GLUTEN-FREE, IF NECESSARY)

½ CUP CHOPPED ALMONDS

⅓ CUP HONEY

¼ CUP UNSALTED BUTTER, CUT INTO PIECES

¼ CUP BROWN SUGAR

¼ TEASPOON KOSHER SALT

1   Coat the Dutch oven lightly with cooking oil.

2   Heat the Dutch oven over a bed of 10 hot coals. Add the oats and almonds, and toast, stirring frequently, until they begin to turn golden brown and become aromatic, about 3 minutes. Transfer the oats and almonds to a bowl.

3   Add the honey, butter, brown sugar, and salt to the Dutch oven and cook over the 10 hot coals, stirring occasionally, until the butter melts and the sugar completely dissolves.

4   Stir the oats and almonds into the butter mixture to combine. Remove the pot from the heat, cover, and allow it to cool to room temperature. When the mixture is firm, cut into bars and serve.

MUSHROOM AND BRIE BREAKFAST STRATA

VEGETARIAN
SOY-FREE
NUT-FREE

SERVES 8

PREP TIME
15 MINUTES

COOK TIME
1 HOUR AND
10 MINUTES

24 COALS

When you are in the mood for a savory breakfast and want to get a bit fancy, this strata recipe is just the thing. It's a hearty casserole made of crusty bread layered with earthy mushrooms and cheese that's baked into a rich custard. Dress it up with fresh or dried herbs, or sautéed onions or shallots.

2 TABLESPOONS COOKING OIL

1 POUND SLICED MUSHROOMS (BUTTON, CREMINI, SHIITAKE, ETC.)

10 LARGE EGGS, LIGHTLY BEATEN

3 CUPS WHOLE MILK OR HALF-AND-HALF

1½ TEASPOONS KOSHER SALT

¾ TEASPOON FRESHLY GROUND BLACK PEPPER

1 (1-POUND) LOAF FRENCH BREAD, CUBED

1 (8-OUNCE) ROUND OF BRIE, RIND REMOVED AND CUT INTO ½-INCH CUBES

1   Heat the oil in the Dutch oven set over 10 hot coals. Add the mushrooms and cook, stirring frequently, until they are softened and beginning to brown, about 10 minutes.

2   While the mushrooms are cooking, in a large bowl, whisk together the eggs, milk or half-and-half, salt, and pepper. Stir in the bread cubes.

3 Remove the Dutch oven from the heat and transfer the mushrooms to a bowl or plate. Pour half of the egg and bread cube mixture into the pot, arranging the bread in an even layer. Top with half of the mushrooms and half of the Brie. Spoon the remaining egg and bread cube mixture over the top. Add the remaining mushrooms and Brie, and then pour the remaining egg mixture over the top. Press down gently to ensure that everything is saturated with the egg mixture.

4 Return the Dutch oven to the bed of 10 hot coals. Cover the pot and place 14 hot coals on the lid. Bake for about 1 hour, until the casserole is puffed up and golden brown. Remove the Dutch oven from the heat and let stand for about 10 minutes before serving.

Camp Hack:

You can mix up the egg and milk or half-and-half mixture ahead of time. Add the bread cubes and store the mixture in a large resealable plastic bag in your cooler overnight (double bag it to prevent leaks). In the morning, you can just cook the mushrooms and layer the ingredients, and the strata will be ready to bake.

Essential Technique:

To easily remove the rind from the Brie, before leaving on your trip, wrap it in plastic wrap and freeze it overnight. Use a serrated knife to slice the rind from the Brie and cut the cheese into cubes. While it's frozen it won't stick to the knife the way refrigerated or room-temperature cheese will.

SAVORY SAUSAGE AND CHEESE FRENCH TOAST CASSEROLE

SOY-FREE
NUT-FREE

SERVES 8

PREP TIME
15 MINUTES

COOK TIME
1 HOUR

24 COALS

This is a more down-home version of the Mushroom and Brie Breakfast Strata (page 54). Using sausage will please carnivores, but you can easily substitute a meatless sausage if you have vegetarians in your group. Again, this is easy to dress up with any seasonings you like. A bit of fresh or dried thyme or oregano, a few spoonfuls of hot salsa, or a diced onion can be sautéed along with the sausage to add flavor.

1 POUND LOOSE BREAKFAST SAUSAGE

8 EGGS

2 CUPS WHOLE MILK

1 TEASPOON KOSHER SALT

½ TEASPOON FRESHLY GROUND
    BLACK PEPPER

2 CUPS (ABOUT 8 OUNCES) SHREDDED SHARP
    CHEDDAR CHEESE

10 TO 12 SLICES SOURDOUGH BREAD

1 Place the Dutch oven over a bed of 10 hot coals. When the pot is hot, add the sausage and cook, stirring frequently and breaking up with a spatula for about 5 minutes, until browned. Transfer the sausage to a plate or bowl. Remove any excess fat from the pot, leaving just about a tablespoon, or enough to coat the bottom and sides of the pot.

2 While the sausage is cooking, whisk together the eggs, milk, salt, and pepper.

3 Remove the Dutch oven from the heat. Arrange half of the bread slices in a single layer in the bottom of the Dutch oven (tear the pieces as needed to fit). Spoon half of the egg mixture over the bread, being sure to saturate each piece of bread. Layer half of the sausage over the bread and sprinkle half of the cheese on top of that. Layer the remaining bread slices over the top. Spoon the remaining egg mixture over the bread, and then layer on the remaining sausage and cheese.

4 Return the Dutch oven to the bed of 10 hot coals, cover the pot, and then place 14 hot coals on the lid. Bake for about 50 minutes, until the cheese is melted and bubbly and the egg mixture is set. Serve hot.

SHAKSHUKA

VEGETARIAN
GLUTEN-FREE
SOY-FREE
NUT-FREE

SERVES 6

PREP TIME
10 MINUTES

COOK TIME
35 MINUTES

26 COALS

This recipe calls for making a quick, chunky, and flavorful tomato sauce and then using the simmering sauce to poach eggs. Serve it with hunks of Crusty No-Knead French Bread (page 148) for sopping up all the delicious sauce. Add a dash of cayenne or hot sauce along with the oregano if you like a bit of a kick.

2 TABLESPOONS OLIVE OIL

1 SMALL ONION, DICED

1 GARLIC CLOVE, MINCED

2 (14-OUNCE) CANS DICED TOMATOES, WITH THEIR JUICE

1 TABLESPOON MINCED FRESH OREGANO OR 1 TEASPOON DRIED OREGANO

1 TEASPOON KOSHER SALT

½ TEASPOON FRESHLY GROUND BLACK PEPPER

6 LARGE EGGS

1   Heat the oil in the Dutch oven set over a bed of 12 hot coals. Add the onion and cook, stirring, for about 4 minutes, until soft. Stir in the garlic and cook 1 more minute. Add the tomatoes, oregano, salt, and pepper and bring to a simmer. Cook, stirring occasionally, until the sauce thickens slightly, about 20 minutes.

2   Crack the eggs into the sauce, spacing them out so that they aren't touching if possible. Cover the pot, place 14 hot coals on the lid, and cook for about 10 minutes, until the egg whites are set but the yolks are still a bit runny. Scoop the eggs, along with a good amount of the sauce, into individual bowls and serve hot.

SWEET POTATO HASH WITH SPICY SAUSAGE

SOY-FREE
NUT-FREE

SERVES 4 TO 6

PREP TIME
10 MINUTES

COOK TIME
30 MINUTES

12 COALS

Variation:
You can substitute
another type of
potato—red, Yukon
Gold, Russet, or Idaho,
for example—for the
sweet potatoes if
you prefer.

Spicy sausage and sweet potatoes are a winning combination. Paired with red bell peppers, sweet onion, and garlic, they make a delicious breakfast hash. If you like, add an egg or two, cooked any way you prefer, to each serving.

1 TABLESPOON COOKING OIL

1 POUND HOT ITALIAN SAUSAGE, SLICED

1 SMALL RED ONION, DICED

2 MEDIUM SWEET POTATOES, PEELED AND DICED

2 GARLIC CLOVES, MINCED

1 RED BELL PEPPER, SEEDED AND DICED

½ TEASPOON KOSHER SALT

½ TEASPOON FRESHLY GROUND BLACK PEPPER

1   Heat the oil in the Dutch oven set over a bed of 12 hot coals. Add the sausage and cook, stirring, for about 4 minutes, until it begins to brown. Add the onions and cook, stirring frequently, for about 4 more minutes, until the onions are soft. Stir in the sweet potatoes, garlic, bell pepper, salt, and pepper

2   Cook, stirring occasionally, for about 20 minutes, until the sweet potatoes are soft and nicely browned. Serve hot.

HASH BROWN–CRUSTED GOAT CHEESE AND SCALLION QUICHE

VEGETARIAN
GLUTEN-FREE
SOY-FREE
NUT-FREE

SERVES 8

PREP TIME
10 MINUTES

COOK TIME
55 MINUTES

26 COALS

Camp Hack:
If you don't want to bother with the crust, you can make this as a crustless quiche. Use just 2 tablespoons of butter, melted in the pot and spread around to coat the bottom and sides, and bake the egg and cheese mixture for about 25 minutes.

Toss the hash browns with melted butter and bake them to a nice crisp before pouring in the egg and cheese filling. You'll end up with a beautiful golden-brown crust for your quiche—a great alternative to pie crust!

¼ CUP UNSALTED BUTTER

3 CUPS, SHREDDED FROZEN HASH BROWNS, THAWED AND DRAINED

6 LARGE EGGS, BEATEN

1½ CUPS WHOLE MILK OR HALF-AND-HALF

6 SCALLIONS, SLICED

1 OUNCE (1½ CUPS) GOAT CHEESE

1 TEASPOON KOSHER SALT

½ TEASPOON FRESHLY GROUND BLACK PEPPER

1 Melt the butter in the Dutch oven over a bed of 12 hot coals. When the butter is melted, remove the pot from the heat and add the hash browns and toss to coat. Press the potatoes into the bottom and up the sides of the pot, creating a crust of even thickness all around. Return the pot to the bed of hot coals, cover, and then place 14 hot coals on the lid. Bake for about 20 minutes. The potatoes will be lightly browned and crisp.

2 While the crust is baking, in a large bowl, whisk together the eggs, milk or half-and-half, scallions, goat cheese, salt, and pepper. Pour the egg mixture into the crust. Remove 2 of the coals from underneath the Dutch oven. Replace the lid and bake with 12 hot coals on the lid for 25 to 30 minutes, until the egg mixture has puffed up and is golden brown on top. Remove from the heat, let cool for a few minutes, and then slice into wedges and serve hot.

SALSA VERDE CHILAQUILES

GLUTEN-FREE
SOY-FREE
NUT-FREE

SERVES 4

PREP TIME
5 MINUTES

COOK TIME
20 MINUTES

26 COALS

This spicy dish is a great way to use up leftover cooked chicken or pork, but it also makes a satisfying vegetarian dish made with beans. Using corn tortilla chips also makes sure that the recipe is gluten-free. Substitute cooked Mexican chorizo for the meat or beans, add scallions or chopped cilantro, or use a red salsa instead of green. As you can see, this is an extremely versatile recipe that you can alter however you like.

2 CUPS SALSA VERDE (CHOOSE HOT, MEDIUM, OR MILD, AS DESIRED)

2/3 CUP SOUR CREAM

3/4 CUP WATER

KOSHER SALT

FRESHLY GROUND BLACK PEPPER

1 (12-OUNCE) BAG CORN TORTILLA CHIPS

2 CUPS COOKED, SHREDDED CHICKEN OR PORK OR 1 (14-OUNCE) CAN PINTO BEANS, DRAINED AND RINSED

4 OUNCES (ABOUT 1 CUP) SHREDDED MONTEREY JACK CHEESE OR OTHER MILD WHITE MELTING CHEESE

1   In a medium bowl, stir together the salsa, sour cream, and water. Add salt and pepper to taste.

2   Put the chips in the Dutch oven and pour the sauce over the top, coating as many of the chips as you can. Top with the shredded meat or beans and then sprinkle the cheese over the top.

3   Cover the Dutch oven with the lid and place it on a bed of 11 hot coals. Place 15 hot coals on the lid. Bake for about 20 minutes, until the whole thing is hot and bubbly and the cheese is melted.

Chapter Four

Chilies, Soups & Stews

THAI CURRY PUMPKIN SOUP

VEGAN
GLUTEN-FREE
SOY-FREE
NUT-FREE

SERVES 6

PREP TIME
5 MINUTES

COOK TIME
15 MINUTES

15 COALS

Variation:
Make this dish more filling by adding a bit of protein such as a can of chickpeas, diced tofu, or cooked chicken breast.

The trick to cooking great food using minimal ingredients is to choose ingredients that deliver layers of flavor. Thai curry paste is a perfect example. In one ingredient, you get the flavors of Thai chilies, garlic, ginger, galangal, lemongrass, kaffir lime, and other ingredients. Curry pastes vary widely by brand in terms of spiciness, so start with the smaller amount and add more to taste.

3 TABLESPOONS COOKING OIL
1 TO 3 TABLESPOONS THAI RED CURRY PASTE
6 CUPS VEGETABLE BROTH
3 (15-OUNCE) CANS PUMPKIN PUREE
1½ (14-OUNCE) CANS COCONUT MILK
KOSHER SALT
¼ CUP CHOPPED CILANTRO

1 Set the Dutch oven over a bed of 15 hot coals. Add the oil and when it begins to simmer, add the curry paste. Cook, stirring, for 1 minute.

2 Add the broth and pumpkin puree, stirring to mix well, and bring to a boil.

3 Stir in the coconut milk and bring to a boil again. Cook for about 10 minutes, stirring frequently and reducing the heat as needed by removing coals from beneath the pot. Taste and add salt as needed. Stir in the cilantro and serve hot.

ITALIAN TOMATO AND ORZO SOUP

VEGAN
SOY-FREE
NUT-FREE

SERVES 6

PREP TIME
5 MINUTES

COOK TIME
25 MINUTES

15 COALS

This rustic Italian-style soup features chunky tomatoes, fresh spinach, and filling pasta. By using canned diced Italian-style tomatoes that are preseasoned with garlic and herbs, you get a flavorful soup with only a handful of ingredients. Garnish with a sprinkling of Parmesan cheese and serve with Crusty No-Knead French Bread (page 148) for dunking, if you like.

2 TABLESPOONS OLIVE OIL

1 ONION, DICED

8 CUPS VEGETABLE BROTH

2 (14-OUNCE) CANS ITALIAN-STYLE DICED
    TOMATOES (WITH GARLIC AND HERBS),
    WITH THEIR JUICE

1 TEASPOON KOSHER SALT

½ TEASPOON FRESHLY GROUND
    BLACK PEPPER

2 CUPS (ABOUT 12 OUNCES) ORZO PASTA, OR
    OTHER SMALL PASTA

4 CUPS (LOOSELY PACKED) SPINACH

1   Set the Dutch oven over a bed of 15 hot coals. Add the oil, and when it begins to simmer, add the onion. Cook, stirring occasionally, until soft, about 5 minutes.

2   Add the broth, tomatoes and their juice, salt, and pepper. Bring to a boil and cook, stirring occasionally, for 10 to 15 minutes.

3   Add the pasta and cook, stirring occasionally, until tender, about 5 to 6 minutes (check the directions on the package). Stir in the spinach and cook until wilted, about 2 more minutes. Serve hot.

BREAD SOUP WITH GREENS

VEGAN
SOY-FREE
NUT-FREE

SERVES 4 TO 6

PREP TIME
5 MINUTES

COOK TIME
35 MINUTES

12 COALS

Variation:
Add a can or two of diced tomatoes (use the type preseasoned with herbs and garlic for added flavor) in addition to or in place of the greens.

Use up your stale bread to make this satisfying soup. The bread thickens the broth, while the beans give it a protein boost. The greens and onions add flavor, color, and nutrients. Substitute chicken broth for the vegetable broth if you like, and top it with a sprinkling of Parmesan cheese.

2 TABLESPOONS OLIVE OIL

1 ONION, DICED

10 TO 12 LEAVES HEARTY GREENS (KALE, CHARD, MUSTARD, ETC.), TOUGH CENTER RIBS REMOVED, LEAVES JULIENNED

1 TEASPOON KOSHER SALT

½ TEASPOON FRESHLY GROUND BLACK PEPPER

1 (14-OUNCE) CAN CANNELLINI BEANS

4 CUPS VEGETABLE BROTH

2 CUPS STALE FRENCH BREAD, CRUSTS REMOVED, TORN OR CUT INTO ½-INCH PIECES

1 Set the Dutch oven over a bed of 12 hot coals and heat the olive oil. Add the onion and cook, stirring frequently, until soft, about 5 minutes. Add the greens, salt, and pepper and cook, stirring, until the greens begin to wilt. If needed to prevent burning, add about ¼ cup of water.

2 Add the beans and broth, and bring to a simmer. Stir in the bread. Cover the pot and remove 2 or 3 of the coals from underneath. Simmer, stirring occasionally, for about 30 minutes, until the bread dissolves into the soup and thickens it. Serve hot.

BUTTERNUT SQUASH AND WHITE BEAN STEW

VEGAN
GLUTEN-FREE
SOY-FREE
NUT-FREE

SERVES 8

PREP TIME
5 MINUTES

COOK TIME
40 MINUTES

12 COALS

Camp Hack:
Leftovers of this stew make a great hash-like base for eggs the next morning. Stir-fry the stew in the Dutch oven or a skillet to heat it and top with fried or poached eggs.

Butternut squash becomes tender, rich, and beautifully sweet when it's cooked in a Dutch oven. Pairing it with tangy tomatoes and hearty beans turns it into a filling meal that will warm you up on a cool evening. For a bit of a kick, add a pinch or two of crushed red pepper flakes along with the salt and pepper. You can also substitute vegetable or chicken broth for the water.

2 TABLESPOONS OLIVE OIL

1 ONION, DICED

2 GARLIC CLOVES, MINCED

4 CUPS CUBED, PEELED BUTTERNUT SQUASH

1 (14-OUNCE) CAN DICED TOMATOES

1 TEASPOON KOSHER SALT

½ TEASPOON FRESHLY GROUND
   BLACK PEPPER

2 CUPS WATER

2 (15-OUNCE) CANS CANNELLINI BEANS,
   DRAINED AND RINSED

1   Heat the oil in the Dutch oven set over a bed of 12 hot coals. Add the onion and cook, stirring frequently, until soft, about 5 minutes.

2   Stir in the garlic, squash, tomatoes, salt, and pepper. Add the water and bring to a simmer. Remove 2 or 3 of the coals underneath the pot, cover, and let simmer for about 25 minutes, until the squash is tender. Stir in the beans and continue to simmer, uncovered, stirring occasionally, until the beans are heated through and the liquid has cooked down a bit, about 10 minutes. Serve hot.

GREEN CHILE AND CORN CHOWDER

VEGETARIAN
GLUTEN-FREE
SOY-FREE
NUT-FREE

SERVES 4

PREP TIME
5 MINUTES

COOK TIME
20 MINUTES

10 COALS

Seasonal Swap:

In the summertime, when fresh corn is at its peak, substitute about 3½ cups (from about 5 ears) of fresh corn kernels for the frozen corn. For extra flavor, steep the cobs in the milk as it cooks, removing them before stirring in the cheese.

This quick and easy vegetarian chowder is full of flavor. You can make it spicy by adding a diced jalapeño or a dash of hot sauce. Frozen corn, once cooked, tastes very much like fresh corn, but you can substitute canned corn if needed. Serve it with a crisp salad and some good bread—try the Crusty No-Knead French Bread (page 148) or the Rosemary Olive Oil Bread (page 152).

1 TABLESPOON OLIVE OIL

1 ONION, CHOPPED

1 (16-OUNCE) PACKAGE FROZEN CORN, THAWED

2 CUPS WHOLE MILK, DIVIDED

1 (14-OUNCE) CAN FIRE-ROASTED DICED GREEN CHILES

¾ TEASPOON KOSHER SALT

1 CUP (ABOUT 4 OUNCES) SHREDDED SHARP CHEDDAR CHEESE, DIVIDED

1 Heat the oil in the Dutch oven set over a bed of 10 hot coals. Add the onion and cook, stirring occasionally, until soft, about 5 minutes. Add the corn and continue to cook for about 3 minutes, until the corn begins to soften. Add the milk, chiles, and salt and bring to a simmer. Cook, stirring frequently, removing coals from underneath the pot if necessary to keep the soup from boiling, until heated through and the corn is very tender, about 10 more minutes

2 Stir in half of the cheese until it is melted and incorporated. Serve hot, garnished with the remaining cheese.

CREAMY SALMON CHOWDER

GLUTEN-FREE
SOY-FREE
NUT-FREE

SERVES 4 TO 6

PREP TIME
5 MINUTES

COOK TIME
30 MINUTES

12 COALS

Smoky bacon provides a deep flavor base for this seemingly decadent chowder. Using canned salmon makes it simple to prepare in the outdoors. As is, it is simple and surprisingly elegant. Dress it up further by adding sliced leeks or celery along with the potatoes, or using chopped fresh chives or parsley as a garnish.

½ POUND SLICED BACON, DICED

½ POUND RED POTATOES, DICED SMALL

1 CUP WATER

3 CUPS HALF-AND-HALF

12 OUNCES CANNED SALMON FILLETS

½ TEASPOON KOSHER SALT

¼ TEASPOON FRESHLY GROUND
   BLACK PEPPER

2 TEASPOONS FRESHLY SQUEEZED
   LEMON JUICE

1   Heat the Dutch oven over a bed of 12 hot coals. Add the bacon and cook, stirring, until the fat is rendered and browned, about 5 minutes. Transfer the bacon to a paper towel–lined plate. Add the potatoes to the bacon fat in the Dutch oven and cook, stirring, until they begin to brown, about 5 minutes. Add the water and cook, stirring occasionally, until the potatoes are tender, about 12 more minutes.

2   Stir in the half-and-half, salmon, salt, and pepper and bring just to a simmer. Remove 2 of the coals from underneath the oven and cook, stirring occasionally, until heated through, about 5 more minutes. Remove pan from the heat. Stir in the lemon juice and serve hot.

FISH STEW WITH TOMATOES

GLUTEN-FREE

SOY-FREE

NUT-FREE

SERVES 4 TO 6

PREP TIME
5 MINUTES

COOK TIME
20 MINUTES

10 COALS

Variation:
You can substitute
peeled shrimp,
squid, scallops, or
other shellfish for
the fish for an even
fancier version. Many
supermarkets sell
frozen mixtures that
would be perfect for
this stew.

This rich stew is deceptively simple to make. The still-frozen fish can be added directly to the simmering broth. If your fish isn't frozen, just reduce the cooking time by 2 or 3 minutes. For an added touch of elegance, mix a minced clove or two of garlic with ½ cup of mayonnaise for a quick aioli and dollop it onto each serving. Serve slices of toasted sourdough bread alongside for dunking into the sauce.

6 TABLESPOONS OLIVE OIL

1 ONION, DICED

1 (14-OUNCE) CAN ITALIAN-STYLE DICED
TOMATOES (WITH GARLIC AND HERBS),
WITH THEIR JUICE

1 CUP DRY WHITE WINE (OR SUBSTITUTE
BROTH OR WATER)

1 CUP WATER

1 TEASPOON KOSHER SALT

½ TEASPOON FRESHLY GROUND
BLACK PEPPER

1½ POUNDS FROZEN FISH FILLETS (ANY MILD
WHITE FISH, SUCH AS COD, HALIBUT, SEA
BASS, OR RED SNAPPER)

1   Heat the olive oil in the Dutch oven set over a bed of 10 hot coals.
    Add the onion and cook, stirring, until soft, about 5 minutes.
    Add the tomatoes, along with their juice, and simmer for about
    10 more minutes.

2   Add the wine (or broth or water), water, salt, pepper, and fish and
    bring to a simmer. Cook, stirring occasionally, until the fish is cooked
    through, about 5 to 7 minutes. Serve hot.

SPICED CHICKPEA
AND POTATO STEW

VEGAN
GLUTEN-FREE
SOY-FREE
NUT-FREE

SERVES 6

PREP TIME
5 MINUTES

COOK TIME
25 MINUTES

10 COALS

Chickpeas are a wonderful camp pantry item. You can toss them into salads, smash them into a spread or dip, or eat them plain as a snack. Here they are cooked with Indian spices and potatoes for a healthy vegetarian meal. You can use any potatoes you have on hand, but my favorite for this dish are Yukon Gold. Add a dollop of plain yogurt and some chopped cilantro as garnishes if you're feeling fancy.

2 TABLESPOONS COOKING OIL

3 SHALLOTS, DICED

1 TABLESPOON GRATED FRESH GINGER

2 CUPS DICED POTATOES

2 TABLESPOONS CURRY POWDER

1 TEASPOON KOSHER SALT

½ TEASPOON FRESHLY GROUND
    BLACK PEPPER

2 (15-OUNCE) CANS CHICKPEAS, DRAINED
    AND RINSED WELL

3 CUPS WATER

1   Heat the oil in the Dutch oven set over a bed of 10 hot coals. Add the shallots and cook, stirring, until soft, about 5 minutes. Stir in the ginger and cook about 1 more minute.

2   Stir in the potatoes, curry powder, salt, and pepper and cook, stirring, for 2 minutes. Add the chickpeas and water. Bring to a simmer. Remove 2 of the coals from underneath the pot and let simmer, uncovered, for about 15 minutes, until the potatoes are tender and the sauce is thick. Serve hot.

VEGAN BLACK BEAN CHILI WITH SWEET POTATOES

VEGAN
GLUTEN-FREE
SOY-FREE
NUT-FREE

SERVES 6

PREP TIME
5 MINUTES

COOK TIME
45 MINUTES

12 COALS

Camp Hack:
If you have leftovers of this chili, it makes a great topping for campfire nachos. Put a bag of tortilla chips in your Dutch oven. Spoon the chili over them, top with shredded cheese, and cook in the covered oven with 10 coals underneath and 12 on top for about 20 minutes, until the cheese is melted and the chili is hot.

Combining canned black beans and sweet potatoes makes a rich, healthy vegan chili that's both sweet and spicy. You can change up the flavor here by varying the type of salsa you use. For instance, use a chipotle salsa for a smoky kick or try one with roasted garlic for added depth of flavor. Serve it with the usual chili toppings—shredded cheese, sour cream, diced avocado, diced jalapeños, sliced scallions.

2 TABLESPOONS OLIVE OIL

2 MEDIUM SWEET POTATOES, PEELED AND DICED

1 TO 2 TABLESPOONS CHILI POWDER

1 TEASPOON KOSHER SALT

½ TEASPOON FRESHLY GROUND BLACK PEPPER

2 CUPS CHUNKY SALSA

2 CUPS VEGETABLE BROTH

2 CUPS WATER

2 (15-OUNCE) CANS BLACK BEANS, DRAINED AND RINSED

1 Heat the oil in the Dutch oven set over a bed of 12 hot coals. Add the sweet potatoes and cook, stirring frequently, until they begin to brown, about 5 minutes. Stir in the chili powder, salt, and pepper and cook, stirring, for 1 minute more. Add the salsa, broth, and water and bring to a boil.

2 Remove 2 of the coals from underneath the pot to reduce the heat. Stir in the beans, cover the pot, and let cook for about 30 minutes, until the sweet potatoes are tender and the broth is thick. Serve hot.

WHITE CHICKEN CHILI

GLUTEN-FREE
SOY-FREE
NUT-FREE

SERVES 6

PREP TIME
5 MINUTES

COOK TIME
15 MINUTES

12 COALS

Make Ahead:
You can roast a chicken before leaving on your trip and use the shredded meat for this recipe. If you really want to save yourself some effort, pick up a rotisserie chicken at the supermarket before you head out.

You'll love how quick and easy this tasty chicken chili is to make. Add your favorite toppings—chopped cilantro, diced avocado, shredded cheese, shredded cabbage, or crumbled tortilla chips—and you can easily have dinner ready in under 30 minutes. You can vary the spice level of the dish by choosing a hotter or milder salsa.

6 CUPS CHICKEN BROTH

4 CUPS COOKED, SHREDDED CHICKEN

2 (15-OZ) CANS WHITE BEANS (SUCH AS CANNELLINI OR GREAT NORTHERN), DRAINED AND RINSED

2 CUPS SALSA VERDE

1 TABLESPOON GROUND CUMIN

KOSHER SALT

1   In the Dutch oven, combine the broth, chicken, beans, salsa, and cumin and set the pot over a bed of 12 hot coals.

2   Bring to a boil, remove 2 or 3 of the hot coals beneath the pot to reduce the heat, cover, and simmer for 10 minutes. Taste and add salt, if needed. Serve hot.

SPICY BEEF AND BEAN CHILI

GLUTEN-FREE
SOY-FREE
NUT-FREE

SERVES 8

PREP TIME
5 MINUTES

COOK TIME
35 MINUTES

12 COALS

This basic chili is always welcome after a day on the trails. It's full of rich flavor, and you can spice it up by adding a pinch of cayenne or a dash of hot sauce. As with the other chilies, it's delicious topped with shredded cheese, sour cream, diced jalapeños, and other toppings. Honey-Sweetened Cornbread (page 143) is the perfect accompaniment.

1 POUND GROUND BEEF

1 ONION, DICED

3 (14-OUNCE) CANS FIRE-ROASTED DICED TOMATOES WITH GREEN CHILES, WITH THEIR JUICE

2 (15-OUNCE) CANS PINTO BEANS, DRAINED AND RINSED

2 TABLESPOONS CHILI POWDER

1 Heat the Dutch oven over a bed of 12 hot coals. Add the beef and onions and cook, stirring frequently and breaking the meat up with a spatula, until the onions are soft and the beef is browned, about 8 minutes. Scoop out any excess fat (leave about 2 tablespoons).

2 Stir in the tomatoes, beans, and chili powder. Cover the pot and remove 2 or 3 coals from underneath to reduce the heat. Simmer for 20 minutes. Remove the lid from the pot and simmer 5 more minutes, until the broth is slightly thickened. Serve hot.

SAUSAGE, BARLEY, AND SPINACH STEW

GLUTEN-FREE
SOY-FREE
NUT-FREE

SERVES 4 TO 6

PREP TIME
5 MINUTES

COOK TIME
25 MINUTES

12 COALS

Italian sausage lends a whole lot of flavor to this simple stew, and you can choose a spicy or mild version depending on your preference. Be sure to use a quick-cooking barley, which cooks in about 10 to 12 minutes, rather than pearled barley, which takes closer to an hour.

1 POUND UNCOOKED ITALIAN SAUSAGE,
    REMOVED FROM CASING

1 ONION, DICED

5 CUPS WATER

2 (14½-OUNCE) CANS ITALIAN-STYLE DICED
    TOMATOES (WITH GARLIC AND HERBS),
    WITH THEIR JUICE

¾ CUP UNCOOKED QUICK-COOKING BARLEY

3 CUPS COARSELY CHOPPED BABY SPINACH

KOSHER SALT

FRESHLY GROUND BLACK PEPPER

1   Heat the Dutch oven over a bed of 12 hot coals. Add the sausage and onions, and cook, stirring frequently and breaking the meat up with a spatula, until the onions are soft and the sausage is browned, about 8 minutes. Scoop out any excess fat (leave about 2 tablespoons).

2   Add the water, tomatoes, and barley to the pot and bring to a boil. Remove 2 to 3 of the hot coals from underneath to reduce the heat. Simmer, uncovered, for 15 minutes, until the barley is tender and the broth has thickened.

3   Stir in the spinach and cook until it wilts, about 1 minute more. Add salt and pepper to taste and serve hot.

SLOW-COOKED BEEF STEW

SOY-FREE
NUT-FREE

SERVES 8

PREP TIME
5 MINUTES

COOK TIME
3 HOURS AND
20 MINUTES

16 COALS, PLUS
ADDITIONAL TO ADD
AS THE ORIGINAL
COALS BURN OUT

Essential Technique:

The trick to a
successful slow-cooked
stew over a campfire
is to stick close to the
fire, keeping an eye
on the dish, stirring as
needed, and adding
hot coals as needed
to keep the heat
level where you need
it. Keep your coal
chimney ready.

*This is a very basic, home-style beef stew recipe that is surprisingly
satisfying to cook and eat around a campfire. The recipe requires very
little in the way of prep, but it's the kind of dish you'll want to make on
a day when you plan to stick around camp all afternoon since it cooks
for several hours.*

2 TABLESPOONS COOKING OIL

3 POUNDS BEEF CHUCK, CUT INTO
1-INCH PIECES

½ CUP ALL-PURPOSE FLOUR

2 (28-OUNCE) CANS DICED TOMATOES WITH
GARLIC AND ONION, WITH THEIR JUICE

2 TEASPOONS KOSHER SALT

1 TEASPOON FRESHLY GROUND
BLACK PEPPER

2 CUPS WATER

1½ POUNDS YUKON GOLD OR OTHER SMALL
POTATOES, QUARTERED

1 (16-OUNCE) BAG FROZEN PEAS AND
CARROTS, THAWED

1   Heat the oil in the Dutch oven set over a bed of 12 hot coals. Toss the
    beef with the flour and season with salt and pepper. Shake off the
    excess and add the beef to the pot and cook, stirring frequently, until
    browned on all sides, about 8 minutes.

2   Add the tomatoes and the salt and pepper.

3 Stir in the water and bring to a boil. Remove 8 coals from beneath the pot, cover, and place 12 hot coals on the lid. Simmer, covered, for 1½ to 2 hours, stirring occasionally and adding a bit of water as needed to prevent sticking or burning. You'll need to keep coals burning alongside your cooking area so that you can add them as the original coals die out.

4 Add the potatoes, replace the lid with the coals on top, and continue to cook for another 45 to 60 minutes, until the meat and potatoes are very tender.

5 Stir in the peas and carrots and cook, stirring, for another 5 to 10 minutes, until the vegetables are tender. Serve hot.

HEARTY GOULASH

GLUTEN-FREE
SOY-FREE
NUT-FREE

SERVES 8

PREP TIME
5 MINUTES

COOK TIME
3 HOURS AND
5 MINUTES

16 COALS, PLUS
ADDITIONAL COALS
AS NEEDED TO
REPLACE COALS AS
THEY BURN OUT

Goulash, a slow-cooked beef stew flavored with lots of paprika, is one of the quintessential Dutch oven campfire dishes. Its origins can be traced back to Hungary in medieval times where it was cooked over an open flame in a cauldron. Although the secret to great goulash is cooking it for hours, it takes very little hands-on prep. And, as with all the dishes in this book, this version requires only 5 ingredients (in addition to staples like salt, pepper, and oil). Serve this with a light salad and Crusty No-Knead French Bread (page 148) for dunking in the sauce.

¼ CUP SWEET PAPRIKA

2 TEASPOONS KOSHER SALT

½ TEASPOON FRESHLY GROUND
    BLACK PEPPER

2 POUNDS BEEF CHUCK ROAST, CUT INTO
    1-INCH CUBES

3 TABLESPOONS OLIVE OIL

1 ONION, CHOPPED

6 CUPS BEEF BROTH

4 CUPS QUARTERED BABY YUKON
    GOLD POTATOES

1   Combine the paprika, salt, and pepper in a large, resealable plastic bag. Add the meat to the bag and shake to coat it well in the seasoning mixture.

2   Heat the oil in the Dutch oven set over a bed of 12 hot coals. Add the onion and cook, stirring frequently, until soft, about 5 minutes.

3 Add the meat and all of the seasoning mixture to the pot and cook, turning the chunks of meat occasionally, until the meat is browned on all sides.

4 Stir in the broth and bring to a boil. Remove 8 coals from beneath the pot, cover the pot, and place 12 hot coals on top. Simmer, covered, for 1½ to 2 hours adding additional coals as needed, and stirring occasionally and adding a bit of water or broth as needed to prevent sticking or burning. You'll need to keep coals burning alongside your cooking area so that you can add them as the original coals die out.

5 Add the potatoes, replace the lid with the coals on top, and continue to cook for another 45 to 60 minutes, until the meat and potatoes are very tender.

Chapter Five

Mains

continued

DUTCH OVEN–BAKED EGGPLANT PARMESAN

VEGETARIAN
SOY-FREE
NUT-FREE

SERVES 4

PREP TIME
10 MINUTES, PLUS
30 MINUTES TO LET
THE EGGPLANT STAND

COOK TIME
35 MINUTES

24 COALS

Essential Technique:
Salting the eggplant
may seem like a
superfluous step,
but it serves to draw
out excess moisture,
including any bitter
flavors, improving
both the taste and
the texture of the
vegetable.

*Many eggplant Parmesan recipes are laborious because they create
way too many dirty dishes for a camping meal. This one is simple. The
eggplant slices are browned in the pot, layered with cheese and tomato
sauce, and then baked until the cheese is melty, the sauce is bubbly, and
the eggplant is meltingly tender.*

1 LARGE EGGPLANT, PEELED AND CUT INTO
   ⅓-INCH-THICK SLICES
1 TEASPOON KOSHER SALT
2 LARGE EGGS, BEATEN
1½ CUPS SEASONED DRY BREAD CRUMBS
¼ CUP OLIVE OIL
3 CUPS MARINARA SAUCE
12 OUNCES SHREDDED ITALIAN CHEESE MIX

1   Arrange the eggplant slices in a single layer on paper towels or in a
    colander. Sprinkle each eggplant slice on both sides with salt. Let the
    salted eggplant stand for 30 minutes. Wipe off the salt and pat the
    eggplant dry with paper towels.

2   Place the eggs in a shallow bowl. Place the breadcrumbs in a separate
    shallow bowl. Dunk each eggplant slice first into the eggs and then
    into the bread crumbs, coating well.

continued

3   Heat the oil in the Dutch oven set over a bed of 12 hot coals. Fry the eggplant slices in batches in the oil until golden brown, about 2 minutes per side. Transfer to a paper towel–lined plate after they are browned.

4   Remove the Dutch oven from the heat and arrange half of the browned eggplant slices in the bottom of the pot. Pour half of the marinara sauce over the layer of eggplant. Sprinkle half of the cheese over the sauce. Repeat, creating another layer with the remaining eggplant, sauce, and cheese.

5   Place the Dutch oven on a bed of 8 hot coals. Cover the pot and place 16 hot coals on the lid. Bake for about 25 minutes, until the sauce is bubbly and the cheese is melted. Serve hot.

THAI BROCCOLI AND CHICKPEA CURRY

VEGAN
GLUTEN-FREE
SOY-FREE
NUT-FREE

SERVES 6 TO 8

PREP TIME
5 MINUTES

COOK TIME
15 MINUTES

12 COALS

Variation:
For added Thai flavor, stir a ½ cup of chopped fresh basil into the curry just before serving.

Curry pastes are a great way to get a lot of flavor into a dish without using a million ingredients. This recipe uses a Thai curry—which includes lemongrass, garlic, ginger, and other Southeast Asian flavors. You could substitute an Indian curry paste for a different flavor. Serve over rice and garnish with chopped cilantro if you've got it.

2 TABLESPOONS COOKING OIL

2 GARLIC CLOVES, MINCED

¼ CUP THAI RED CURRY PASTE

2 HEADS BROCCOLI, CUT INTO FLORETS

2 (15-OUNCE) CANS COCONUT MILK

2 (14-OUNCE) CANS CHICKPEAS, DRAINED AND RINSED

1 TABLESPOON CORNSTARCH DISSOLVED IN ¼ CUP COLD WATER

1   Heat the oil in the Dutch oven set over a bed of 12 hot coals. Add the garlic and cook, stirring frequently, until soft, about 3 minutes. Stir in the curry paste and cook 1 more minute. Add the broccoli and cook, stirring, for 2 to 3 minutes, and then add the coconut milk. Cook until the broccoli is tender, about 3 more minutes.

2   Add the chickpeas and bring back to a boil. Stir in the cornstarch mixture and cook, stirring, for another minute or 2 until the sauce thickens. Serve hot.

CAMPFIRE MAC AND CHEESE

VEGETARIAN
SOY-FREE
NUT-FREE

SERVES 6 TO 8

PREP TIME
5 MINUTES

COOK TIME
10 MINUTES

8 COALS

Camp Hack:
Precook the macaroni at home and pack it in a large resealable plastic bag in your cooler.

Variation:
Use any good melting cheese you like or, even better, a mixture of two or more such as sharp Cheddar and American, or Fontina and Gruyère.

This is one of the quickest ways to make mac and cheese, and it's really not that much more difficult than preparing the boxed version. Using evaporated milk gives you a thick, rich sauce without bothering with a roux. You can add whatever you like into the mix for added flavor. Crumbled bacon, toasted bread crumbs, diced jalapeños, frozen corn or peas, blanched broccoli florets, or chunks of ham are all favorites.

½ CUP (1 STICK) UNSALTED BUTTER

2 LARGE EGGS

1 (12-OUNCE) CAN EVAPORATED MILK

2 TEASPOONS KOSHER SALT

1 TEASPOON FRESHLY GROUND
    BLACK PEPPER

1½ POUNDS SHREDDED CHEESE

1 (16-OUNCE) PACKAGE MACARONI, COOKED
    ACCORDING TO PACKAGE DIRECTIONS

1 Melt the butter in the Dutch oven set over a bed of 8 hot coals. In a bowl, whisk together the eggs, milk, salt, and pepper. Whisk the egg mixture into the melted butter.

2 Add the cheese and the pasta and cook, stirring constantly, until the pasta is heated through and the sauce is thick and creamy, about 3 minutes. Serve hot.

CARAMELIZED ONION AND GRUYÉRE PASTA BAKE

SERVES 6

PREP TIME
10 MINUTES

COOK TIME
1 HOUR AND
10 MINUTES

28 COALS

Make Ahead:
You can caramelize
the onions at home
to save time at the
campsite. Store them
in a resealable plastic
bag or lidded plastic
container in your
cooler until you're
ready to cook.

This one-pot pasta dish coaxes deep flavor out of a few onions, and then adds flavorful cheese and rich cream for what is really a grown-up version of mac and cheese. Add a bit of dry mustard, cayenne, or other spices along with the salt and pepper. You can also infuse the pasta with fresh herbs, like thyme or rosemary, by adding a sprig or two along with the water and pasta.

¼ CUP (½ STICK) UNSALTED BUTTER

3 SWEET ONIONS, HALVED AND
   THINLY SLICED

1 TEASPOON KOSHER SALT

½ TEASPOON FRESHLY GROUND
   BLACK PEPPER

4¾ CUPS WATER

1 (16-OUNCE) PACKAGE SHORT-CUT PASTA
   (PENNE, SHELLS, FUSILLI, ETC.)

1¼ CUPS HEAVY CREAM

10 OUNCES GRUYÉRE CHEESE, SHREDDED

1   Melt the butter in the Dutch oven over a bed of 12 hot coals. Add the onions, salt, and pepper. Cook, stirring frequently, until they are soft and golden brown, 15 to 20 minutes.

continued

2 Add the water and pasta, and stir to mix. Remove 4 of the coals from underneath the pot, cover the pot, and place 20 hot coals on the lid. Bake for about 40 minutes, until the pasta is tender.

3 Remove the lid, stir in the cream and half of the cheese, and cook, stirring, for about 2 minutes, until the cheese is melted. Sprinkle the remaining cheese over the top, move the pot off the bed of coals and replace the lid, including the hot coals. Broil for about 4 more minutes, until the cheese on top is melted. Serve hot.

SPINACH AND CHEESE LASAGNA

VEGETARIAN
SOY-FREE
NUT-FREE

SERVES 6

PREP TIME
10 MINUTES

COOK TIME
1 HOUR

28 COALS, PLUS
ADDITIONAL AS
NEEDED TO REPLACE
COALS AS THEY
BURN OUT

Lasagna is the ultimate comfort food, and even more so on a cool night in the outdoors. Using no-boil lasagna noodles, a good quality jarred pasta sauce, and a shredded Italian cheese blend makes this dish as easy to prep as it is satisfying. Serve it cut into wedges with garlic bread and salad.

1 TABLESPOON OLIVE OIL

1 (24-OUNCE) JAR PASTA SAUCE

1 (16-OUNCE) PACKAGE NO-BOIL
   LASAGNA NOODLES

3 CUPS FRESH BABY SPINACH

2 CUPS SHREDDED ITALIAN-STYLE
   CHEESE BLEND

1 TABLESPOON DRIED ITALIAN
   SEASONING BLEND

1   Coat the bottom of the Dutch oven with the oil and then spread ½ cup of the sauce over the bottom. Create a layer of noodles, arranging them so they don't overlap. Top with another ½ cup of sauce, 1 cup of the spinach, and ½ cup of the cheese. Add two more layers of noodles, sauce, spinach, and cheese. Finish with a layer of noodles, the remaining sauce, and the remaining ½ cup of cheese. Sprinkle with the Italian seasoning.

2   Cover the Dutch oven and place it on a bed of 8 hot coals. Top the pot with 20 hot coals. Bake for about 50 to 60 minutes until the noodles become tender and the cheese melts. You'll need to keep coals burning alongside your cooking area so that you can add them as the original coals die out.

DUTCH OVEN–PIZZA MARGHERITA

VEGETARIAN
SOY-FREE
NUT-FREE

SERVES 4

PREP TIME
5 MINUTES

COOK TIME
25 MINUTES

35 COALS

High temperature is a crucial element for making a good pizza. Using a cast iron Dutch oven over a fire is one of the best ways to ensure you have the high heat you need, short of installing a wood-burning brick pizza oven. This is a simple pizza recipe that uses canned sauce and store-bought dough for convenience. Of course, you can make your own sauce and dough if you are motivated. There's plenty of room here for variation. Just add whatever toppings you like.

1 (14- TO 16-OUNCE) PACKAGE REFRIGERATED
   PIZZA DOUGH, AT ROOM TEMPERATURE
1 (7-OUNCE) CAN OF PIZZA SAUCE
2 CUPS SHREDDED MOZZARELLA CHEESE
¼ CUP JULIENNED FRESH BASIL LEAVES

1   Press the pizza dough into a flat round, about the same size as the bottom of the Dutch oven (12 inches).

2   Lightly oil the Dutch oven and press the pizza dough round into it. Spread the sauce onto the dough.

3 Place the Dutch Oven over a bed of 15 hot coals, cover the pot, and place 20 hot coals on the lid. Bake for 15 minutes, until the edge of the dough begins to brown. Add the cheese, sprinkling it in an even layer over the sauce, replace the lid with the coals on top, and continue to bake for 5 to 10 more minutes, until the cheese is melted and bubbly.

4 Sprinkle the basil over the top, remove from the Dutch oven, and slice into wedges. Serve hot.

Camp Hack:

The hardest part of this recipe may be getting the hot pizza out of the very hot Dutch oven. To make it easier, before putting the dough into the Dutch oven, make a sling out of aluminum foil. The edges of the sling should hang over the sides of the pot. Use this sling to lift the cooked pizza out of the oven.

Variation:

Add any of your favorite pizza toppings: sliced pepperoni, crumbled Italian sausage, diced bell peppers, caramelized onions, sliced mushrooms, or chopped fresh herbs.

ROASTED COD WITH OLIVES, LEMON, AND CAPERS

GLUTEN-FREE
SOY-FREE
NUT-FREE

SERVES 4

PREP TIME
5 MINUTES

COOK TIME
15 MINUTES

34 COALS

Seasonal Swap:
In the summertime, when tomatoes are at their peak, add a pint of halved cherry tomatoes along with the olives.

A meaty white fish like cod is the perfect match for the Dutch oven. Add just a few flavorful ingredients—like lemon, capers, and olives— and you've got a flavorful and healthy meal in 20 minutes. Add a side of couscous or quinoa and a green salad for a simple, but satisfying dinner.

4 (6-OUNCE) COD FILLETS

KOSHER SALT

FRESHLY GROUND BLACK PEPPER

12 THIN LEMON SLICES

¼ CUP PITTED, CHOPPED KALAMATA OLIVES

¼ CUP CAPERS, DRAINED AND CHOPPED

2 TEASPOONS CHOPPED FRESH ROSEMARY LEAVES

¼ CUP OLIVE OIL

1 Arrange the fish fillets in a single layer in the Dutch oven and season with salt and pepper. Top each piece of fish with 3 lemon slices and then scatter the olives, capers, and rosemary evenly over the top. Drizzle the olive oil evenly over all of the fish. Place the lid on the pot.

2 Place the Dutch oven on a bed of 10 hot coals and then place 24 hot coals on the lid. Cook for about 15 minutes, until the fish is cooked through. Serve hot.

BUTTER AND GARLIC BAKED SHRIMP

GLUTEN-FREE
SOY-FREE
NUT-FREE

SERVES 4 TO 6

PREP TIME
5 MINUTES

COOK TIME
15 MINUTES

16 COALS

Camp Hack:
Buy frozen, raw, peeled, and deveined shrimp rather than peeling them yourself at camp. Put the frozen shrimp in your cooler and they'll keep other items cold, too. If necessary, submerge the bag in a bowl of cold water to thaw before cooking.

It takes only a few minutes to throw this dish together, but it tastes more like something you'd get at a nice restaurant than at a campsite. This is a dish you'll definitely want to serve with warm, Crusty No-Knead French Bread (page 148) for dunking so you don't lose any of the buttery, garlicky sauce.

¼ CUP (½ STICK) UNSALTED BUTTER

2½ POUNDS SHRIMP, PEELED AND DEVEINED

6 GARLIC CLOVES, MINCED

JUICE OF 1 LARGE LEMON

¼ CUP WHITE WINE (OR SUBSTITUTE BROTH OR WATER)

1 CUP CHOPPED TOMATOES

½ TEASPOON KOSHER SALT

½ TEASPOON FRESHLY GROUND BLACK PEPPER

1 Melt the butter in the Dutch oven place on a bed of 6 hot coals. Add the shrimp, garlic, lemon juice, wine (or broth or water), tomatoes, salt, and pepper and cover the pot.

2 Add 20 hot coals to the lid and bake for about 10 minutes, until the shrimp are cooked through. Serve hot.

MANGO SHRIMP

NUT-FREE

SERVES 4

PREP TIME
5 MINUTES

COOK TIME
10 MINUTES

10 COALS

Camp Hack:
Use frozen mango that comes already chopped to save time. The bag of frozen fruit will help keep your cooler chilled, too.

Mango and lime juice give this simple shrimp dish tropical flare. Serve it over plain rice or, better yet, rice cooked with coconut milk. To make it a bit spicy, add a teaspoon of crushed red chiles or garlic-chili paste along with the soy sauce.

2 TABLESPOONS COOKING OIL

1 LARGE ONION, CHOPPED

2 MEDIUM MANGOS, CUBED

¼ CUP SOY SAUCE

JUICE OF 2 LIMES

2 POUNDS PEELED AND DEVEINED SHRIMP

1   Heat the oil in the Dutch oven set over a bed of 10 hot coals. Add the onion and cook, stirring, until soft and beginning to brown, about 5 minutes.

2   Add the mango, soy sauce, lime juice, and shrimp and cook, stirring occasionally, until the shrimp are cooked through, about 5 more minutes. Serve hot.

CRISPY BEER-BATTERED FRIED FISH

SOY-FREE
NUT-FREE

SERVES 4 TO 6

PREP TIME
10 MINUTES

COOK TIME
10 MINUTES

14 COALS

Essential Technique:
Before adding the breaded fish, test your oil to make sure it is hot enough. Drop a few flecks of the batter into the oil. It should sizzle and immediately begin to brown.

The Dutch oven is great for deep-frying, and I much prefer to make this dish outdoors rather than splatter oil all over my kitchen stovetop. Choose any beer you enjoy drinking for this recipe, and be sure to have extra on hand for washing down these crispy, salty strips of fried fish. Serve with coleslaw or a green salad for a delicious dinner.

COOKING OIL FOR FRYING, ABOUT 4 CUPS

1 (12-OUNCE) CAN BEER (LAGER-STYLE)

2 CUPS ALL-PURPOSE FLOUR, DIVIDED

½ TEASPOON KOSHER SALT, PLUS ADDITIONAL FOR SEASONING

2 POUNDS COD FILLETS, CUT DIAGONALLY INTO 1-INCH WIDE BY 5- OR 6-INCH LONG STRIPS

MALT VINEGAR, FOR SERVING

1   Fill the Dutch oven about ½ full with oil and place it over a bed of 14 hot coals. Heat until the oil is very hot.

2   To make the batter, whisk together the beer and 1½ cups of the flour in a large bowl until well combined. Stir in the ½ teaspoon of salt. Place the remaining ½ cup of flour in a wide, flat bowl.

3   Pat the fish dry with paper towels and season on both sides with salt and pepper. Dunk each piece of fish in the batter, dredge it in the flour, and lower it gently into the Dutch oven. Cook several pieces of fish at a time, but be careful not to crowd the pot. Turn the fish pieces frequently as they cook, until they turn a deep golden brown, about 5 minutes. Transfer the cooked fish to a paper towel–lined plate and season with salt. Serve immediately with malt vinegar for sprinkling over the top.

BALSAMIC-BRAISED CHICKEN

GLUTEN-FREE
SOY-FREE
NUT-FREE

SERVES 6 TO 8

PREP TIME
5 MINUTES

COOK TIME
50 MINUTES

14 COALS

Camp Hack:
If peeling and chopping garlic at camp seems too laborious, save yourself the time and effort by bringing along a jar of minced garlic. A teaspoon of the jarred stuff is equal to about 1 garlic clove.

Braising chicken in sweet-and-sour balsamic vinegar infuses it with intense flavor, which is balanced by a touch of sweet honey and rich tomato paste. Serve this saucy chicken with Parmesan Garlic Potatoes (page 127). For a special touch, garnish the dish with sliced scallions or chopped fresh parsley.

2 TABLESPOONS COOKING OIL

3 POUNDS BONELESS, SKINLESS CHICKEN THIGHS

1 TEASPOON KOSHER SALT

¾ TEASPOON FRESHLY GROUND BLACK PEPPER

3 GARLIC CLOVES, MINCED

1 (6-OUNCE) CAN TOMATO PASTE

½ CUP WATER

⅔ CUP BALSAMIC VINEGAR

3 TABLESPOONS HONEY

1   Heat the oil in the Dutch oven set over a bed of 14 hot coals. Season the chicken all over with salt and pepper, and cook it (in batches if necessary) in the Dutch oven, turning once, until browned on both sides, about 6 minutes. Remove the chicken from the pot as it is browned and transfer it to a plate.

2 Add the chopped the garlic and cook, stirring, for 1 minute. Stir in the tomato paste and water, and cook, stirring and scraping up the browned bits from the bottom of the pot, for about 2 minutes. Add the vinegar and honey. Bring to a boil.

3 Return the chicken to the pot and remove 6 of the coals from underneath the pot. Cook, turning the chicken occasionally, until the chicken is very tender and cooked through and the sauce has thickened to a syrupy consistency, about 30 to 40 minutes. If the sauce isn't thick enough, transfer the chicken to a plate when it is cooked, add 6 hot coals underneath the pot, bring to a boil, and cook, stirring, until the sauce thickens. Return the chicken to the pot until heated through. Serve hot.

CHICKEN BRAISED IN COCONUT MILK WITH BASIL

GLUTEN-FREE
SOY-FREE
NUT-FREE

SERVES 6

PREP TIME
5 MINUTES

COOK TIME
1 HOUR AND
15 MINUTES

26 COALS, PLUS
ADDITIONAL AS
NEEDED TO REPLACE
COALS AS THEY
BURN OUT

Variation:
For additional
flavor, add some
fish sauce, thinly
sliced lemongrass
stalks, scallions,
and/or cilantro. Add
vegetables like green
beans, broccoli, or
cauliflower after the
dish has been baking
for about 40 minutes
and serve over rice to
make it a full meal.

This simple braised chicken takes on intense richness due to the coconut milk and the long, slow cooking process. It's delicious as is, with just a few ingredients, but you can vary it with any number of flavorful additions. I like to add a couple of sliced fresh red chiles (serrano or jalapeño peppers).

2 TABLESPOONS COOKING OIL

1 TABLESPOON BUTTER

3 POUNDS BONELESS, SKINLESS
    CHICKEN THIGHS

KOSHER SALT

FRESHLY GROUND BLACK PEPPER

8 GARLIC CLOVES, PEELED AND LEFT WHOLE

1 (14-OUNCE) CAN COCONUT MILK

½ CUP CHOPPED FRESH BASIL

1   Heat the oil and butter in the Dutch oven set over 14 hot coals. Season the chicken pieces generously with salt and pepper, and add them to the pot, browning them (in batches if needed to avoid crowding the pan). Cook, turning once, until browned on both sides, about 6 minutes. Transfer the chicken pieces to a plate as they are browned.

2   Add the garlic to the pot and cook, stirring, for 1 minute. Add the coconut milk and return the chicken, along with any accumulated juices, to the pot. Cover the pot. Remove 8 of the coals from beneath the pot and place 20 hot coals on the lid. Bake for about 1 hour, until the chicken is fall-apart tender. Remove from the heat and stir in the basil. Serve hot.

WHOLE ROAST CHICKEN
WITH ROOT VEGETABLES

GLUTEN-FREE
SOY-FREE
NUT-FREE

SERVES 4 TO 6

PREP TIME
10 MINUTES

COOK TIME
1 HOUR AND
40 MINUTES

24 COALS, PLUS
ADDITIONAL AS
NEEDED TO REPLACE
COALS AS THEY
BURN OUT

A whole chicken roasted in a pot with potatoes, carrots, and onions is a beautiful thing—especially when it's cooked over a campfire. It is a complete meal on its own and oh so satisfying. Add a chilled glass of dry white wine and, for me at least, it just might be the most perfect camping meal.

¼ CUP OLIVE OIL

1 WHOLE (3- TO 4-POUND) CHICKEN

KOSHER SALT

FRESHLY GROUND BLACK PEPPER

6 GARLIC CLOVES, PEELED AND LEFT WHOLE

2 ONIONS, CUT INTO RINGS

1 POUND SMALL RED OR YELLOW POTATOES,
    HALVED OR QUARTERED

4 CARROTS, PEELED AND CUT INTO
    2-INCH PIECES

1   Heat the oil in the Dutch oven set over 8 hot coals. Season the chicken generously all over with salt and pepper, and place it in the Dutch oven, breast side down. Cook for about 6 minutes, until browned. Turn the chicken over and brown the other side for about 6 minutes. Remove the chicken from the oven and place it on a plate.

continued

2 Add the garlic, onions, potatoes, and carrots to the Dutch oven and toss with the oil. Season with additional salt and pepper. Spread the vegetables out into an even layer and then place the chicken on top, breast side up. Settle the chicken onto the vegetables so that it sits nicely in the middle of the pot.

3 Cover the pot and place 16 hot coals on the lid. Cook for 1 hour, checking to make sure the coals are still hot and adding additional coals as needed. Check the chicken for doneness (165°F on a meat thermometer or when the juices run clear when you cut into it) after an hour and continue to cook until it is fully cooked, which could take up to an additional 30 minutes. Serve the chicken hot, along with the cooked vegetables.

Camp Hack:

Make your chicken even more flavorful by rubbing it all over with a dry spice rub (I like a combo of paprika, garlic powder, onion powder, salt, pepper, and thyme) before leaving home. Pack it well to avoid leakage. Note that the chicken likely won't need to be seasoned again with salt and pepper since your spice rub will already contain these.

CHICKEN PARMESAN

SOY-FREE
NUT-FREE

SERVES 4

PREP TIME
10 MINUTES

COOK TIME
40 MINUTES

26 COALS

Camp Hack:
If you didn't flatten your chicken breasts at home, pop them into resealable plastic bags and use a wine bottle, beer bottle, can of tomatoes, or any other heavy, cylindrical object you happen to have handy to pound them flat.

Using a good marinara sauce, seasoned bread crumbs, and a mix of Italian cheeses gives this dish plenty of flavor without going over the 5-ingredient limit. I like to serve this crispy, saucy chicken sandwich-style on crusty sourdough rolls, but it also goes well with pasta, or even a plain green salad.

3 TABLESPOONS OLIVE OIL

1 LARGE EGG, BEATEN

4 BONELESS, SKINLESS CHICKEN BREAST
HALVES, POUNDED FLAT

KOSHER SALT

FRESHLY GROUND BLACK PEPPER

1 CUP SEASONED BREAD CRUMBS

1½ CUPS SHREDDED CHEESE SUCH AS
MOZZARELLA OR AN ITALIAN CHEESE MIX

2 CUPS MARINARA SAUCE

1 Heat the oil in the Dutch oven set over a bed of 8 hot coals.

2 In a bowl, whisk the egg. Season the chicken pieces generously with salt and pepper. Next, dunk them into the egg, and then into the bread crumbs.

continued

3 Add the coated chicken pieces to the pot and cook until golden brown on both sides, about 4 minutes per side. Remove the chicken pieces as they are browned and place them on a plate.

4 When all of the chicken pieces are browned, remove any excess oil from the pot and add half of the marinara sauce. Arrange the browned chicken pieces on top and pour the remaining sauce over the top. Sprinkle the cheese over the top. Cover the pot and add 18 hot coals to the lid. Bake for about 30 minutes, until the chicken is cooked through, the sauce is bubbling, and the cheese is melted. Serve immediately.

GINGER-SOY CHICKEN

NUT-FREE

SERVES 4 TO 6

PREP TIME
5 MINUTES

COOK TIME
1 HOUR AND
10 MINUTES

10 COALS, PLUS
ADDITIONAL AS
NEEDED TO REPLACE
COALS AS THEY
BURN OUT

Variation:
You can make this dish even more flavorful by adding a cinnamon stick, a piece of dried star-anise, and a couple of chopped scallions along with the ginger and garlic.

This is a simplified version of a classic Cantonese dish. The sweet-salty glaze on the tender chicken is addictive. The side ideas are endless. Some of my favorites are steamed broccoli and grilled asparagus. Serve it over rice with the sauce spooned on top.

3 POUNDS SKIN-ON, BONE-IN CHICKEN THIGHS

1 CUP SOY SAUCE

3 CUPS WATER

1 (2-INCH) PIECE GINGER, PEELED AND
    THINLY SLICED

3 GARLIC CLOVES, CRUSHED

3 TABLESPOONS SUGAR

1   Place the chicken in the Dutch oven and add the soy sauce and water. The water should come about ¾ of the way up the sides of the chicken, so add additional water if needed. Set the pot over a bed of 10 hot coals and bring to a boil. Immediately remove 4 to 6 of the coals so that the liquid is just simmering.

2   Stir in the ginger, garlic, and sugar and simmer for 45 to 60 minutes, until the chicken is very tender and the liquid has thickened. Add additional coals as needed to keep the liquid at a simmer. Serve hot.

COCONUT THAI CURRY CHICKEN

GLUTEN-FREE
SOY-FREE
NUT-FREE

SERVES 4 TO 6

PREP TIME
5 MINUTES

COOK TIME
25 MINUTES

12 COALS

Variation:
For added flavor, use fish sauce instead of salt and/or stir in the juice of 1 lime and ½ cup chopped fresh basil or cilantro just before serving.

Chicken braised in a broth made of coconut milk and flavorful Thai red curry paste is easy to make but full of enticing Southeast Asian flavor. Serve it with grilled vegetables and white or brown rice for a complete meal that is healthy and satisfying.

2 TABLESPOONS COOKING OIL

1 ONION, DICED

1 TO 3 TABLESPOONS THAI RED CURRY PASTE

1 (14-OUNCE) CAN COCONUT MILK

2 CUPS WATER

1 TABLESPOON BROWN SUGAR

1½ POUNDS BONELESS, SKINLESS CHICKEN THIGHS

KOSHER SALT

FRESHLY GROUND BLACK PEPPER

1 Heat the oil in the Dutch oven set over 12 hot coals. Add the onion and cook, stirring, until soft, about 5 minutes. Add the curry paste and cook, stirring, for 1 to 2 more minutes, until it just begins to brown.

2 Stir in the coconut milk, water, brown sugar, chicken, salt, and pepper and bring to a boil. Remove 4 of the coals from underneath the pot and let simmer until the chicken is tender and cooked through, about 15 minutes. Serve hot.

CHICKEN POT PIE WITH BISCUIT TOPPING

SOY-FREE
NUT-FREE

SERVES 6

PREP TIME
15 MINUTES

COOK TIME
30 MINUTES

24 COALS

Variation:
Use a premade piecrust in place of the biscuits (substitute ¼ cup all-purpose flour for the ¼ cup of baking mix and eliminate ½ cup of the butter, ½ cup of the milk, and the baking mix).

Chicken pot pie is one of my favorite foods. It's so homey and comforting, and really hits the spot when you're camping someplace with chilly evenings. It's a great way to use up any leftover cooked chicken.

¾ CUP (1½ STICKS) COLD UNSALTED BUTTER, DIVIDED

2¼ CUPS ALL-PURPOSE BAKING MIX (PAGE 42), OR STORE-BOUGHT BAKING MIX, DIVIDED

2 CUPS CHICKEN BROTH

1¼ CUPS MILK, DIVIDED

1 POUND BAG FROZEN MIXED VEGETABLES (CARROTS, CORN, PEAS)

1½ POUNDS (ABOUT 3 CUPS) COOKED, DICED CHICKEN

1 Melt ¼ cup of the butter in the Dutch oven set over 14 hot coals. Sprinkle in ¼ cup of the baking mix and cook, stirring constantly, until it just begins to brown, about 5 minutes.

2 Add the chicken broth, ¾ cup of the milk, the vegetables, and the chicken and stir to mix. Let simmer until the sauce thickens, about 5 more minutes.

continued

3 Meanwhile, combine the remaining 2 cups of baking mix with the remaining ½ cup of butter (cut into small pieces) in a medium bowl, rubbing them together with your hands until the mixture resembles coarse meal. Stir in the remaining ½ cup of milk until a soft dough forms. Press the dough out into a round shape about the size of the Dutch oven.

4 Remove 8 of the coals from underneath the pot. Place the dough round on top of the chicken and sauce mixture. Cover the pot and place 18 hot coals on the lid. Bake for about 20 minutes, until the crust is flaky and golden brown. Serve hot.

SPICY SAUSAGE JAMBALAYA

GLUTEN-FREE
SOY-FREE
NUT-FREE

SERVES 4 TO 6

PREP TIME
5 MINUTES

COOK TIME
1 HOUR AND
10 MINUTES

28 COALS, PLUS
ADDITIONAL AS
NEEDED TO REPLACE
COALS AS THEY
BURN OUT

Camp Hack:
Topped with a fried egg, leftover jambalaya makes a great breakfast the next morning.

Jambalaya is a hearty one-pot rice dish that's easy to make. This version uses spicy sausage and Cajun seasoning for lots of flavor. I like andouille sausage, but you can substitute any smoked, spicy sausage you like.

1 TABLESPOON COOKING OIL

1½ POUNDS SLICED ANDOUILLE SAUSAGE

1 ONION, DICED

1 CUP RICE

1 TEASPOON CAJUN SEASONING

1 (14-OUNCE) CAN DICED TOMATOES, WITH
    THEIR JUICE

2 CUPS WATER

1   Heat the oil in the Dutch oven set over a bed of 8 hot coals. Add the sausage and cook, stirring occasionally, until it begins to brown, about 4 minutes. Add the onion and cook, stirring frequently, until the sausage browns and the onion softens, about 5 more minutes.

2   Add the rice and stir to coat. Stir in the seasoning, tomatoes along with their juice, and the water. Cover the pot and place 20 hot coals on the lid. Bake for about 1 hour, checking occasionally and adding additional water as needed, until the rice is tender. You'll need to keep coals burning alongside your cooking area so that you can add them as the original coals die out. Serve hot.

ONE-POT SPAGHETTI IN MEAT SAUCE

SOY-FREE
NUT-FREE

SERVES 6

PREP TIME
5 MINUTES

COOK TIME
40 MINUTES

24 COALS

Cooking and draining pasta at a campsite can be a bit of a hassle, but here the pasta is cooked right in the sauce for a true one-pot spaghetti dinner. Using Italian-style diced tomatoes, preseasoned with garlic and herbs, gives you lots of classic Italian flavor without having to bring your whole spice cabinet along.

1½ POUNDS LEAN GROUND BEEF

1 ONION, DICED

1 TEASPOON KOSHER SALT

2 GARLIC CLOVES, MINCED

2 (28-OUNCE) CANS ITALIAN-STYLE DICED TOMATOES (WITH GARLIC AND HERBS), WITH THEIR JUICE

1 (16-OUNCE) PACKAGE SPAGHETTI, BROKEN IN HALF

1   Heat the Dutch oven set over a bed of 8 hot coals. Add the beef and cook, stirring and breaking up with a spatula, until the meat is browned. Stir in the onion, salt, and garlic. Cook, stirring, until the onion is soft, about 5 more minutes.

2   Stir in the tomatoes, along with their juice, and the spaghetti and bring to a simmer. Cover the pot and place 16 hot coals on the lid. Cook for 20 to 30 minutes, checking after 15 minutes and adding a bit of water if needed, until the pasta is tender. Serve hot.

CITRUS CHIPOTLE ROAST PORK

GLUTEN-FREE
SOY-FREE
NUT-FREE

SERVES 8

PREP TIME
5 MINUTES

COOK TIME
1 HOUR AND
10 MINUTES

25 COALS, PLUS
ADDITIONAL TO
REPLACE COALS AS
THEY BURN OUT

Variation:
You can make this with any cut of pork you like. A loin or tenderloin will make a nice, lean roast. Pork shoulder has more fat and therefore will be more flavorful, but it may need to cook a bit longer.

Sweet and tangy orange and lime juice mixed with spicy and smoky chipotle chiles in adobo sauce give this pork roast its intense flavor. The pork can marinate for up to 2 days, so this is a great recipe to prep at home (put the meat and marinade in a large resealable plastic bag) and bring along to cook on day two or three.

1 CUP FRESHLY SQUEEZED ORANGE JUICE

½ CUP FRESHLY SQUEEZED LIME JUICE

1 CHIPOTLE CHILE IN ADOBO, PLUS
    2 TABLESPOONS OF THE SAUCE FROM
    THE JAR

2 GARLIC CLOVES, MINCED

KOSHER SALT

FRESHLY GROUND BLACK PEPPER

1 (2-POUND) BONELESS PORK ROAST

2 TABLESPOONS COOKING OIL

1 In a large bowl or resealable plastic bag, combine the orange juice, lime juice, chipotle chile and adobo sauce, garlic, salt, and pepper. Add the pork and turn to coat. Let marinate in the cooler for at least an hour. Remove the bag from the cooler about 30 minutes before beginning to cook so that it can come to room temperature.

2 Heat the oil in the Dutch oven set over 12 hot coals. Remove the roast from the marinade, reserving the extra liquid, and brown on all sides in the Dutch oven, about 10 minutes total.

continued

3 Add the reserved marinade, cover the pot. Remove 4 coals from underneath the pot and place 17 hot coals on the lid. Cook for about 30 minutes, then check the roast and turn it over. Continue to cook, adding additional coals as needed, to maintain a simmer for another 15 to 30 minutes, until the pork is cooked through.

4 Remove the roast from the oven, tent with foil, and let rest for at least 10 minutes before slicing. If desired, let the marinade simmer and thicken in the pot while the meat rests. Carve the roast into ¼-inch-thick slices and serve with the thickened marinade spooned over the top.

CIDER AND DIJON ROAST PORK

GLUTEN-FREE
SOY-FREE
NUT-FREE

SERVES 6

PREP TIME
5 MINUTES

COOK TIME
40 MINUTES

25 COALS

Variation:
Add a peeled and diced green apple along with the onion to add even more tart and sweet apple flavor.

Braising pork tenderloin in tart and sweet apple cider flavors the meat and keeps it moist and tender. Serve it with mashed, baked, or roasted potatoes and grilled asparagus or zucchini for a very civilized fireside meal.

3 TABLESPOONS OLIVE OIL, DIVIDED

2 PORK TENDERLOINS (ABOUT
    2½ POUNDS TOTAL), EACH CUT
    INTO 2 PIECES

KOSHER SALT

FRESHLY GROUND BLACK PEPPER

1 LARGE ONION, CHOPPED

½ CUP DRY WHITE WINE (OR SUBSTITUTE
    BROTH OR WATER)

1 TABLESPOON DIJON MUSTARD

1 CUP APPLE CIDER

1   Heat the oil in the Dutch oven set over 12 hot coals. Season the pork generously with salt and pepper, and sear it in the oil until browned on all sides, about 8 minutes. Transfer to a plate.

2   Add the onion to the pot and cook, stirring frequently, until soft, about 5 minutes. Add the wine (or broth or water) to the pot and cook, stirring, until it has reduced a bit, about 3 minutes. Return the pork to the pot, along with any juices that have accumulated on the plate. Spread the mustard over the pork and pour the cider over the top. Cover the pot.

continued

3 Remove 5 coals from underneath the pot and place 18 hot coals on the lid. Cook for about 25 minutes, until the pork is cooked through. Remove from the heat and let the pork rest for about 10 minutes. Carve into ¼-inch-thick slices and serve with the onions and sauce spooned over the top.

SAUSAGE BRAISED WITH APPLES AND CABBAGE

GLUTEN-FREE
SOY-FREE
NUT-FREE

SERVES 4

PREP TIME
5 MINUTES

COOK TIME
1 HOUR AND
30 MINUTES

24 COALS, PLUS
ADDITIONAL TO
REPLACE COALS AS
THEY BURN OUT

This easy-prep dish is always a winner. Everything goes in the pot at once and it cooks with little attention. The result is a sweet and savory combo of tender cabbage, sweet apples, and smoky sausage that only needs a hunk of bread or some mashed or roasted potatoes to round out the meal. You can use any sausage you like for this dish.

1 POUND SMOKED SAUSAGE, SLICED IN ½-INCH PIECES

½ HEAD CABBAGE, COARSELY CHOPPED

1 ONION, SLICED

1 LARGE GRANNY SMITH APPLE, PEELED, CORED, AND COARSELY CHOPPED

¼ CUP (PACKED) BROWN SUGAR

1 TEASPOON SALT

½ TEASPOON FRESHLY GROUND BLACK PEPPER

½ CUP WATER

1   Heat the Dutch oven over a bed of 6 hot coals and add the sausage. Cook, stirring, until it begins to brown, about 5 minutes. Add the cabbage, onion, apple, brown sugar, salt, pepper, and water. Cover the pot and add 18 hot coals to the lid.

2   Bake for 1 hour to 1 hour and 30 minutes, until the cabbage and apples are very tender and the mixture is hot and bubbly. You'll need to keep coals burning alongside your cooking area so that you can add them as the original coals die out. Serve hot.

SEARED NEW YORK STRIP STEAK IN MUSHROOM CREAM SAUCE

GLUTEN-FREE
SOY-FREE
NUT-FREE

SERVES 2 TO 3

PREP TIME
5 MINUTES

COOK TIME
20 MINUTES

10 COALS

Essential Technique:

Always let meat rest for 5 to 10 minutes after cooking and before serving. This allows the meat to reabsorb the juices it releases when its hot. It also gives the proteins a chance to relax. The result is a juicy, tender piece of meat.

Camping dining doesn't get much better than steak seared in a cast iron pan. That is, until you spoon a rich cream sauce over the top. This recipe serves 2 to 3 people but is easily doubled, either by using 2 Dutch ovens to cook the steaks or by doing them in batches (you can make the doubled sauce in one pot).

1 TABLESPOON OLIVE OIL

2 NEW YORK STRIP STEAKS (ABOUT 8 OUNCES EACH)

KOSHER SALT

FRESHLY GROUND BLACK PEPPER

¼ CUP MINCED SHALLOTS

6 OUNCES SLICED MUSHROOMS

¼ CUP DRY WHITE WINE (OR SUBSTITUTE BROTH OR WATER)

¼ CUP WATER

¼ CUP CRÈME FRAÎCHE OR SOUR CREAM

1   Heat the oil in the Dutch oven set over 10 hot coals. Season the steaks generously with salt and pepper, and add to the pot. Cook, turning once, until browned on the outside and medium-rare in the center, about 8 minutes. Transfer the browned steaks to a plate.

2 Drain excess oil from the pot, leaving about 1 tablespoon. Add the shallots and mushrooms and cook, stirring, until soft, about 8 minutes. Add the wine (or broth or water) and cook, stirring and scraping up the browned bits from the bottom of the pan, for about 2 minutes. Add the water and crème fraîche or sour cream to the pot and cook, stirring, until the sauce thickens slightly, about 2 more minutes. Serve the steaks with the sauce spooned over the top.

GARLICKY POT ROAST

GLUTEN-FREE
SOY-FREE
NUT-FREE

SERVES 6 TO 8

PREP TIME
5 MINUTES

COOK TIME
1 HOUR AND
25 MINUTES

24 COALS, PLUS
ADDITIONAL TO
REPLACE COALS AS
THEY BURN OUT

A Dutch oven is the ideal vessel for cooking something like beef chuck roast that needs long, slow cooking in a moist environment. The carrots, wine, and broth add the moisture, while smashed garlic permeates the meat with flavor. Serve this hearty dish with foil-wrapped potatoes baked in the coals beneath the pot.

2 TABLESPOONS OLIVE OIL

1 (3-POUND) BONELESS BEEF CHUCK ROAST

KOSHER SALT

FRESHLY GROUND BLACK PEPPER

1 CUP DRY RED WINE

1 CUP BEEF OR CHICKEN BROTH

4 CARROTS, PEELED AND CUT INTO
    2-INCH PIECES

8 GARLIC CLOVES, SMASHED

1   Rub the olive oil all over the roast. Season the roast generously with salt and pepper.

2   Heat the Dutch oven over a bed of 10 hot coals. Add the roast and cook until browned on all sides, about 10 minutes.

3   Add the wine, broth, carrots, and garlic to the pot, distributing the vegetables around the roast. Cover the pot and remove 3 of the coals from underneath. Add 17 hot coals to the top of the pot. Cook for 1 hour to 1 hour and 15 minutes, until the roast is very tender. You'll need to keep coals burning alongside your cooking area so that you can add them as the original coals die out. Remove the roast from the pot and put it on a serving platter or plate, cover with aluminum foil and let stand for 10 minutes before serving. To serve, slice and serve hot, along with the carrots and juices from the pot.

CLASSIC MEATLOAF

SOY-FREE
NUT-FREE

SERVES 4 TO 6

PREP TIME
5 MINUTES

COOK TIME
1 HOUR

24 COALS, PLUS
ADDITIONAL TO
REPLACE COALS AS
THEY BURN OUT

Camp Hack:
Use leftovers to make
sandwiches for lunch
the next day. Serve
on whole wheat bread
with mayonnaise
and lettuce.

This simple version of an American comfort food classic delivers plenty of flavor with just a few ingredients. Serve it with steamed green beans and mashed potatoes for a campsite meal that tastes like the epitome of home cooking. I find that this easy "meat and potatoes meal" is surprisingly satisfying as a camp dinner.

1 TABLESPOON COOKING OIL

1½ POUNDS LEAN GROUND BEEF

1 TEASPOON KOSHER SALT

½ TEASPOON FRESHLY GROUND
   BLACK PEPPER

½ ONION, FINELY MINCED

1 LARGE EGG, BEATEN

½ CUP BREAD CRUMBS

¾ CUP KETCHUP, DIVIDED

1 Coat the bottom of the Dutch oven with the oil. If using tin foil, layer it on the bottom of the Dutch oven and coat with a light layer of oil.

2 In a large bowl, mix together the beef, salt, pepper, onion, egg, bread crumbs, and ¼ cup of the ketchup. Transfer the mixture to the Dutch oven and form it into a flat, round loaf in the center of the pot with space around the sides. Cover the top of the meatloaf with the remaining ½ cup of ketchup. Cover the pot.

3 Place the Dutch oven over a bed of 9 hot coals, cover the pot, and place 15 hot coals on the lid. Cook for 45 to 60 minutes, until the meatloaf is cooked through. You'll need to keep coals burning alongside your cooking area so that you can add them as the original coals die out. Remove from the heat and let stand for 5 to 10 minutes before slicing and serving.

Chapter
Six

Sides & Snacks

CREAMY POLENTA WITH CORN

VEGETARIAN
GLUTEN-FREE
SOY-FREE
NUT-FREE

SERVES 8

PREP TIME
5 MINUTES

COOK TIME
1 HOUR

24 COALS, PLUS
ADDITIONAL TO
REPLACE COALS AS
THEY BURN OUT

Camp Hack:
Scramble any leftovers
with eggs for breakfast
the next morning for a
filling meal.

Polenta is a welcome change from the usual pasta or rice. This version skips the constant stirring required by most recipes. The polenta is instead baked at moderate heat for about an hour until it is creamy and thick. Top it with tomato sauce or meat sauce if you like.

¼ CUP (1 STICK) UNSALTED BUTTER,
    PLUS ADDITIONAL FOR PREPARING
    THE DUTCH OVEN

2 CUPS UNCOOKED POLENTA (COARSELY
    GROUND YELLOW CORNMEAL)

2 CUPS FROZEN CORN KERNELS

2 TEASPOONS KOSHER SALT

1 TEASPOON FRESHLY GROUND
    BLACK PEPPER

1 CUP FRESHLY GRATED PARMESAN CHEESE

4 OUNCES CREAM CHEESE

1 Coat the inside of the Dutch oven lightly with butter. Add the polenta, corn, salt, and pepper, and stir to mix. Cover the Dutch oven and place it over a bed of 6 hot coals. Place 18 hot coals on the lid. You'll need to keep coals burning alongside your cooking area so that you can add them as the original coals die out. Bake for 45 minutes.

2 Remove the lid and stir in the Parmesan cheese, cream cheese, and the remaining butter. Replace the lid, including the hot coals, and bake for another 15 minutes. Serve hot.

SWEET AND SAVORY BOURBON BAKED BEANS

GLUTEN-FREE
SOY-FREE
NUT-FREE

PREP TIME
5 MINUTES

COOK TIME
1 HOUR AND
25 MINUTES

24 COALS, PLUS
ADDITIONAL TO
REPLACE COALS AS
THEY BURN OUT

I happen to think one should always have a bottle of bourbon on hand for camping, and this recipe provides the perfect excuse to tuck one into your supply box. These beans make a great side dish to any barbecued meat, but frankly the dish is so satisfying that I'm happy to eat it for dinner—especially if I have a piece of Honey-Sweetened Cornbread (page 143) to dunk into the sauce.

4 OUNCES THICK-CUT BACON, DICED

1 CUP (PACKED) BROWN SUGAR

½ CUP SPICY MUSTARD

1¼ CUPS WATER

⅔ CUP BOURBON

3 (15-OUNCE) CANS NAVY OR GREAT
    NORTHERN BEANS, DRAINED AND RINSED

KOSHER SALT

FRESHLY GROUND BLACK PEPPER

1 Heat the Dutch oven over a bed of 10 hot coals. Add the bacon and
   cook, stirring frequently, until browned, about 6 minutes. Transfer
   the bacon to a paper towel–lined plate and drain excess fat from the
   pot, leaving just about 2 tablespoons.

continued

2   Add the brown sugar, mustard, water, and bourbon to the Dutch oven and bring to a boil. Cook, stirring frequently, until the sugar dissolves. Stir in the beans, salt, and pepper and cover the pot. Remove 4 of the coals from beneath the pot and add 18 hot coals to the lid. Cook, stirring occasionally and adding a bit of additional water if needed, until the sauce is thick, 45 to 60 minutes. You'll need to keep coals burning alongside your cooking area so that you can add them as the original coals die out.

3   Add the cooked bacon, stirring to mix, and continue to cook, covered, for about 15 more minutes. Serve hot.

MEXICAN BEANS AND RICE

VEGAN
GLUTEN-FREE
SOY-FREE
NUT-FREE

SERVES 4 TO 6

PREP TIME
5 MINUTES

COOK TIME
25 MINUTES

24 COALS

Salsa gives this dish its spicy Mexican flavor. You can use whatever kind of salsa you like, choosing one with a spice level that suits you. Serve this as a side dish to grilled chicken or steak, or use it as the primary component for a burrito, along with shredded cheese, diced avocados, and shredded lettuce.

1 TABLESPOON OLIVE OIL

1 CUP LONG-GRAIN WHITE RICE

2 TEASPOONS CHILI POWDER

1 TEASPOON CUMIN

1 (15-OUNCE) CAN PINTO BEANS, DRAINED
    AND RINSED

1½ CUPS SALSA

1½ CUPS WATER

1 TEASPOON KOSHER SALT

½ TEASPOON FRESHLY GROUND
    BLACK PEPPER

1   Heat the oil in the Dutch oven over a bed of 10 hot coals. Stir in the rice and cook, stirring, for 1 minute. Add the chili powder and cumin, and cook for another 30 seconds. Stir in the beans, salsa, water, salt, and pepper.

2   Cover the Dutch oven and remove 4 of the coals from underneath the pot and place 18 hot coals on the lid. Cook for about 20 minutes, until the rice is tender and most of the liquid has been absorbed. Serve hot.

PARMESAN RISOTTO

VEGETARIAN
GLUTEN-FREE
SOY-FREE
NUT-FREE

SERVES 6 TO 8

PREP TIME
5 MINUTES

COOK TIME
40 MINUTES

25 COALS

Seasonal Variation:
In the springtime, try adding asparagus spears cut into 2-inch pieces along with the broth.

This risotto is baked over the coals and doesn't require constant stirring, but you'll be surprised by how creamy and tender it becomes. Serve this as a side dish to grilled or roasted meat, fish, or chicken. Better yet, stir cooked shrimp, leftover cooked chicken, or steak into the mix along with the cheese in the final step to make it a meal.

¼ CUP OLIVE OIL
2 GARLIC CLOVES, MINCED
2 CUPS ARBORIO RICE
6 CUPS VEGETABLE (OR CHICKEN) BROTH
1¼ CUPS GRATED PARMESAN CHEESE
KOSHER SALT
FRESHLY GROUND BLACK PEPPER

1   Heat the olive oil in the Dutch oven set over 8 hot coals. Add the garlic and cook, stirring, for 1 minute. Stir in the rice until the grains are coated with the oil. Add the broth and cover the pot with the lid. Place 17 hot coals on the lid and bake for about 35 minutes, until the rice is tender.

2   Remove the lid and stir in the cheese. Taste and add salt and pepper as needed.

RICE PILAF WITH DRIED APRICOTS AND ALMONDS

VEGAN
GLUTEN-FREE
SOY-FREE

SERVES 6 TO 8

PREP TIME
5 MINUTES

COOK TIME
30 MINUTES

23 COALS

Camp Hack:
Bring along extra dried apricots and almonds. They make a great snack, either while you cook or to bring along on a hike.

This rice pilaf, studded with sweet dried apricots and crunchy almonds, is a big step up from plain rice, but is almost as easy to make. Feel free to substitute any other dried fruit, such as raisins or cranberries, for the apricots. Serve it as a side dish with any type of grilled meat, fish, tofu, or vegetables.

3 TABLESPOONS OLIVE OIL

1 ONION, DICED

2 CUPS LONG-GRAIN RICE

4 CUPS VEGETABLE (OR CHICKEN) BROTH OR WATER

½ CUP CHOPPED DRIED APRICOTS

½ CUP SLICED ALMONDS

1 Heat the olive oil in the Dutch oven set over 12 hot coals. Add the onion and sweat, stirring frequently, until soft, about 5 minutes. Add the rice and cook, stirring, until it begins to brown, about 3 minutes. Add the broth or water and dried apricots, and stir to mix.

2 Cover the pot and remove 5 of the coals. Add 16 hot coals to the lid. Cook for about 20 minutes, until the rice is cooked through and most of the liquid has been absorbed.

3 Stir in the almonds and let stand for a few minutes before serving.

BALSAMIC ROASTED VEGETABLES

VEGAN
GLUTEN-FREE
SOY-FREE
NUT-FREE

SERVES 6

PREP TIME
10 MINUTES

COOK TIME
40 MINUTES

32 COALS

Camp Hack:
Leftover roasted vegetables make a great base for a breakfast frittata. They can also be added to sandwiches or tossed into a salad.

Roasting vegetables caramelizes their sugars and gives them depth of flavor that you can't get with any other cooking method. Adding a bit of balsamic vinegar and Dijon mustard gives them even more flavor. Serve these as a side dish to any type of grilled meat, sausage, or fish.

2 TABLESPOONS BALSAMIC VINEGAR

1 TEASPOON DIJON MUSTARD

½ CUP OLIVE OIL

1 TEASPOON KOSHER SALT

½ TEASPOON FRESHLY GROUND
   BLACK PEPPER

3 GARLIC CLOVES, PRESSED

2 LARGE RED ONIONS, HALVED AND THINLY
   SLICED

2½ TO 3 POUNDS CHOPPED OR CUBED
   VEGETABLES (ANY COMBINATION OF
   GREEN, YELLOW, RED, OR ORANGE BELL
   PEPPERS; EGGPLANT; OR ZUCCHINI OR
   OTHER SUMMER SQUASH)

1   In a medium bowl, whisk together the vinegar and mustard. Whisk in the oil, salt, and pepper.

2   Combine the garlic, onions, and vegetables in the Dutch oven. Drizzle the balsamic mixture over the top and toss to coat. Cover the Dutch oven.

3   Set the Dutch oven on a bed of 8 hot coals. Add 24 hot coals to the lid. Roast for 30 to 35 minutes, until the vegetables are tender and lightly browned. Serve hot.

PARMESAN GARLIC POTATOES

VEGETARIAN
GLUTEN-FREE
SOY-FREE
NUT-FREE

SERVES 6

PREP TIME
10 MINUTES

COOK TIME
1 HOUR AND
15 MINUTES

26 COALS, PLUS
ADDITIONAL TO
REPLACE COALS AS
THEY BURN OUT

Variation:
You can use russet
or Idaho potatoes
here, but you may
want to peel them
before slicing.

Speckled with bits of garlic and Parmesan cheese, these crispy potatoes are a delightful cross between tender baked potatoes, crispy roasted potatoes, and cheesy garlic fries. Really, you can serve them as a side dish to just about any meal and they'll be scarfed up immediately, but they make an especially apt partner to Seared New York Strip Steak in Mushroom Cream Sauce (page 114).

3 TABLESPOONS OLIVE OIL, DIVIDED

6 LARGE RED OR YUKON GOLD POTATOES,
    THINLY SLICED, VERTICALLY, MOST OF THE
    WAY THROUGH

6 TABLESPOONS UNSALTED BUTTER, CUT INTO
    SMALL PIECES

6 GARLIC CLOVES, MINCED

KOSHER SALT

FRESHLY GROUND BLACK PEPPER

½ CUP FRESHLY GRATED PARMESAN CHEESE

1 Coat the bottom and sides of the Dutch oven with 1 tablespoon of the olive oil.

2 Arrange the potato slices vertically in the Dutch oven, drizzle the remaining 2 tablespoons of olive oil over the top, dot with the butter, and then sprinkle with the garlic, salt, pepper, and Parmesan cheese.

3 Cover the pot and place it on a bed of 6 hot coals. Place 20 hot coals on the lid. Bake for 1 hour to 1 hour and 15 minutes, until the potatoes are cooked through and crisp. You'll need to keep coals burning alongside your cooking area so that you can add them as the original coals die out. Serve hot.

CREAMY MASHED POTATOES WITH GREEK YOGURT

VEGETARIAN
GLUTEN-FREE
SOY-FREE
NUT-FREE

SERVES 6

PREP TIME
10 MINUTES

COOK TIME
35 MINUTES

22 COALS

Mashed potatoes go great with all kinds of grilled meats and vegetables, and they're easy to make. The Dutch oven will keep them warm throughout the meal as well. These are made with Greek yogurt instead of cream, which gives them a tangy flavor and makes them lighter than the classic versions. Feel free to add a few spoonfuls of goat cheese or blue cheese, substitute sour cream for the yogurt, or spice the recipe up with a dash of cayenne or diced chiles.

5 POUNDS RED POTATOES, QUARTERED
¾ CUP PLAIN GREEK YOGURT
2 TABLESPOONS UNSALTED BUTTER
KOSHER SALT

1   Put the potatoes in the Dutch oven and cover with water. Set the Dutch oven over a bed of 14 hot coals and bring to a boil. Remove 8 of the coals from underneath the pot, cover, and simmer for about 30 minutes, until the potatoes are tender.

2   Remove the oven from the heat. Drain the potatoes and return them to the Dutch oven. Mash the potatoes with a large fork or potato masher. Add the butter and mash it into the potatoes as it melts. Stir in the yogurt and salt to taste. Serve hot.

CRISPY SPICED SWEET POTATO FRIES

VEGAN
GLUTEN-FREE
SOY-FREE
NUT-FREE

SERVES 6

PREP TIME
5 MINUTES

COOK TIME
20 MINUTES

16 COALS

Variation:

For extra crispy fries, soak the sweet potato sticks in water for 30 minutes, then drain and let dry in a colander for 1 hour before cooking.

Every camping trip should include a burger night—whether you serve veggie burgers, turkey burgers, or classic beef burgers. Serve these tasty spiced sweet potato fries alongside for an unforgettable meal. These fries are also welcome by themselves as an afternoon snack. Dip them in ketchup, salsa, or Queso Fundido with Chorizo (see recipe on page 133).

1 TABLESPOON CHILI POWDER

2 TEASPOONS GROUND CUMIN

1 TEASPOON KOSHER SALT

1 TEASPOON GARLIC POWDER

COOKING OIL FOR FRYING, ABOUT 4 CUPS

3 MEDIUM SWEET POTATOES, PEELED AND CUT INTO ¼-INCH-WIDE STICKS

1 In a small bowl, stir together the chili powder, cumin, salt, and garlic powder.

2 Fill the Dutch oven with about 3 inches of cooking oil and heat it over a bed of 16 hot coals until the oil is very hot.

3 Drop the fries into the hot oil in batches, and cook, turning occasionally, until they are golden brown all over, about 5 minutes. As each batch is finished cooking, transfer them to a paper towel–lined plate and sprinkle with some of the spice mixture. Serve immediately.

CORN FRITTERS

VEGETARIAN
SOY-FREE
NUT-FREE

SERVES 6

PREP TIME
5 MINUTES

COOK TIME
15 MINUTES

16 COALS

Seasonal Swap:
In the summertime, when corn is at its peak, use fresh kernels cut straight from the cob for this dish.

Crispy corn fritters make a delicious snack or side dish, and the Dutch oven is the perfect vessel to fry them in. The trick to making them crisp and not too greasy is to make sure the oil is very hot before you start frying them. Drop a bit of the batter in to test it—it should sizzle and begin to brown immediately.

1 CUP FROZEN CORN KERNELS

1 EGG, SEPARATED

¼ CUP MILK

⅔ CUP ALL-PURPOSE FLOUR

½ TEASPOON BAKING POWDER

¼ TEASPOON SALT

COOKING OIL FOR FRYING, ABOUT 4 CUPS

1 In a medium bowl, combine the corn, egg yolk, milk, flour, baking powder, and salt. Stir to mix well.

2 In a large bowl, beat the egg white until stiff peaks form. Fold the egg white into the corn mixture.

3 Fill the Dutch oven with about 3 inches of cooking oil and heat it over a bed of 16 hot coals until the oil is very hot.

4 Drop the batter into the hot oil by heaping spoonfuls and cook, turning over once, until the fritters are golden brown all over, about 4 minutes. Cook the fritters in batches to avoid crowding the pot, and transfer the cooked fritters to a paper towel-lined plate. Serve immediately.

GOAT CHEESE–STUFFED MUSHROOMS

VEGETARIAN
SOY-FREE
NUT-FREE

SERVES 6

PREP TIME
10 MINUTES

COOK TIME
20 MINUTES

28 COALS

Warm goat cheese-stuffed mushrooms topped with crispy bread crumbs make an elegant appetizer or a hearty snack. I love the combination of herbes de Provence *(usually a blend of thyme, savory, marjoram, rosemary, and other herbs) with the goat cheese, but you can use any dried herb or herb blend you like.*

1½ TEASPOONS *HERBES DE PROVENCE* OR ITALIAN HERB SEASONING

¼ CUP BREAD CRUMBS

1½ TABLESPOONS UNSALTED BUTTER, AT ROOM TEMPERATURE

18 WHOLE CREMINI MUSHROOMS (ABOUT 8 OUNCES), STEMS REMOVED

4 OUNCES GOAT CHEESE

1 TABLESPOON OLIVE OIL

1½ TEASPOONS BALSAMIC VINEGAR

½ TEASPOON KOSHER SALT

½ TEASPOON FRESHLY GROUND BLACK PEPPER

1 In a small bowl, mix together the *herbes de Provence*, bread crumbs, and butter.

2 In a medium bowl, toss together the mushrooms, oil, vinegar, salt, and pepper.

continued

3   Spoon the goat cheese into the individual mushrooms, dividing evenly. Top each filled mushroom with about ½ tablespoon of the bread crumb mixture and arrange the filled mushrooms in a single layer in the Dutch oven. Cover the Dutch oven with the lid.

4   Place the Dutch oven over a bed of 8 hot coals. Place 20 hot coals on the lid. Bake for about 20 minutes, until the mushrooms are tender and the topping is browned and crisp. Serve hot.

QUESO FUNDIDO WITH CHORIZO

SOY-FREE
NUT-FREE

SERVES 6

PREP TIME
5 MINUTES

COOK TIME
20 MINUTES

18 COALS

With molten cheese and spicy Mexican sausage, this dip is always a crowd pleaser. It's also easy to vary to suit your personal taste. For instance, you can add diced jalapeños or use pepper Jack cheese if you prefer a spicier version. Or add mild green chiles for flavor without the kick. Open a bag of tortilla chips and watch this dip disappear in minutes.

4 OUNCES CHORIZO, CASING REMOVED

½ SMALL ONION, FINELY DICED

1 RED BELL PEPPER, SEEDED AND DICED

8 OUNCES SHREDDED MONTEREY
    JACK CHEESE

3 SCALLIONS, THINLY SLICED

1 Heat the Dutch oven over a bed of 8 hot coals. Add the chorizo and onion, and cook, stirring, until the sausage is browned and the onion is soft, about 5 minutes. Drain excess fat from the pot. Remove 2 of the coals from underneath the pot.

2 Stir in the bell pepper and cheese, and place the lid on the Dutch oven. Place 12 hot coals on the lid and cook for 10 to 15 minutes, until the cheese is melted and bubbly. Sprinkle the sliced scallions over the top and serve hot, with tortilla chips for dipping.

KETTLE CORN

VEGAN
GLUTEN-FREE
SOY-FREE
NUT-FREE

SERVES 6

PREP TIME
5 MINUTES

COOK TIME
10 MINUTES

8 COALS

Popcorn is always a fun snack, but this salty-sweet kettle corn is completely addictive. Be warned that the pot will be very hot, so good heatproof gloves are a must. Keep children away while this is cooking, but watch them dive in with gusto once it's finished.

⅓ CUP COOKING OIL

1 CUP POPCORN KERNELS

½ CUP SUGAR

1 TEASPOON KOSHER SALT

Essential Technique:
The trick to cooking kettle corn in a Dutch oven is to wait to add the sugar until the popcorn is almost all popped. This way you avoid burning the sugar.

1   Heat the oil in the Dutch oven over a bed of 8 hot coals. After the oil has been heating for a minute or two, add a few popcorn kernels. When those kernels pop, add the remaining kernels. Cover the pot, and when the popcorn begins to pop, shake the pot (protecting your hands with heatproof gloves). Let cook for about 30 seconds, then shake for about 30 seconds. Cook for about 3 to 5 minutes, until the popping sounds have slowed down.

2   Carefully lift the lid and add the sugar, sprinkling it over the popcorn. Replace the lid and cook, shaking the pot continuously, for 1 to 2 more minutes. Transfer the popcorn to a large bowl, sprinkle with the salt, and serve immediately.

MINI BEAN AND CHEESE QUESADILLAS

VEGETARIAN
SOY-FREE
NUT-FREE

SERVES 8

PREP TIME
15 MINUTES

COOK TIME
15 MINUTES

15 COALS

These crispy mini quesadillas make a fun afternoon snack, or even a main course. They're easy to make and kids love them. Serve them with additional toppings if you like, such as sour cream, guacamole, sliced scallions, or chopped cilantro.

½ CUP REFRIED BEANS

2 TEASPOONS CHILI POWDER

2 CUPS SHREDDED CHEESE, SUCH AS A
MEXICAN CHEESE BLEND OR PEPPER JACK

24 ROUND WONTON WRAPPERS

2 TABLESPOONS COOKING OIL

SALSA FOR SERVING

1 In small bowl, stir together the beans, chili powder, and cheese. Spoon about 1 tablespoon of the mixture onto each wonton wrapper, spreading it over 1 half of the wrapper. Fold the wrappers over the filling. Dip a fingertip into a small bowl of water and run it around the edges to help seal.

2 Heat the cooking oil in the Dutch oven set over 15 hot coals. Arrange several of the quesadillas in the pan in a single layer. Cook for 1 to 2 minutes per side, until the wrappers are browned and crisp, and the filling is melted. Drain on a paper towel–lined plate. Serve hot, with salsa for dipping.

Chapter Seven

Breads & Rolls

CHEESY BISCUITS

VEGETARIAN
SOY-FREE
NUT-FREE

MAKES 12 BISCUITS

PREP TIME
10 MINUTES

COOK TIME
25 MINUTES

24 COALS

Variation:
For extra flavor,
add fresh or dried
herbs, diced hot or mild
chiles, crumbled bacon,
or other flavorful
ingredients along with
the cheese.

This recipe uses the All-Purpose Baking Mix (page 42) to make basic, flaky biscuits that are loaded with cheesy goodness. Eat them hot, spread with butter or honey, for a snack or serve them as a side dish to soup or stew.

½ CUP (1 STICK) COLD UNSALTED BUTTER,
    CUT INTO SMALL PIECES, PLUS
    ADDITIONAL FOR PREPARING THE
    DUTCH OVEN

2 CUPS ALL-PURPOSE BAKING MIX (PAGE 42),
    OR STORE-BOUGHT BISCUIT MIX

½ CUP MILK

1 CUP (ABOUT 4 OUNCES) SHREDDED SHARP
    CHEDDAR CHEESE

1   Lightly coat the Dutch oven with butter. Place the Dutch oven over a bed of 6 hot coals, cover the pot, and place 18 hot coals on the lid.

2   In a medium bowl, combine the baking mix with the butter and use your fingers to work it into the dry ingredients until the mixture resembles a coarse meal. Add the milk and cheese, and stir to mix well, until you have a thick dough. Add additional milk, if needed, to thin the dough or additional baking mix to thicken it.

3   Form the dough into 12 balls of roughly equal size and flatten each ball into a patty. Arrange the patties in the preheated Dutch oven in a single layer. Cover the Dutch oven (you should still have 18 hot coals on the lid) and bake for 20 to 25 minutes, rotating the pot by a quarter turn every few minutes, until the biscuits are golden brown on the outside. Serve warm.

CORNMEAL AND HONEY BISCUITS

VEGETARIAN
SOY-FREE
NUT-FREE

MAKES 12 BISCUITS

PREP TIME
10 MINUTES

COOK TIME
25 MINUTES

24 COALS

Variation:
To give the biscuits
a lustrous sheen,
brush the tops with
additional buttermilk
before baking.

These slightly sweet biscuits get extra flavor and texture from cornmeal that is added to the All-Purpose Baking Mix (page 42). These are the perfect side dish for a spicy chili, and they also make a great snack or breakfast.

½ CUP (1 STICK) COLD BUTTER, CUT INTO
    SMALL PIECES, PLUS ADDITIONAL FOR
    PREPARING THE DUTCH OVEN

1½ CUPS ALL-PURPOSE BAKING MIX (PAGE 42),
    OR STORE-BOUGHT BISCUIT MIX

¾ CUP CORNMEAL

2 TEASPOONS BAKING POWDER

¾ TEASPOON KOSHER SALT

1 CUP BUTTERMILK

3 TABLESPOONS HONEY

1   Lightly coat the Dutch oven with butter. Place the Dutch oven over a bed of 6 hot coals, cover, and place 18 hot coals on the lid.

2   In a medium bowl, combine the baking mix with the cornmeal, baking powder, and salt. Add the ½ cup of butter and use your fingers to work it into the dry ingredients until the mixture resembles a coarse meal. Stir in the buttermilk and honey until well combined. Reserve a little bit of the buttermilk on the side.

continued

3 Form the dough into 12 balls of roughly equal size and flatten each ball into a patty. Arrange the patties in the preheated Dutch oven in a single layer. Cover the Dutch oven (you should still have 18 hot coals on the lid) and bake for 20 to 25 minutes, rotating the pot by a quarter turn every few minutes, until the biscuits are golden brown on the outside.

4 Bake for about 15 minutes, or until nicely browned on top. Serve warm.

SIMPLE BANANA BREAD

VEGETARIAN
SOY-FREE
NUT-FREE

SERVES 8

PREP TIME
5 MINUTES

COOK TIME
40 MINUTES

23 COALS

Variation:
Stir in a cup of chopped nuts (pecans, walnuts, or hazelnuts) and/or a cup of semisweet chocolate chips just before transferring the batter to the Dutch oven.

Banana bread makes a great snack—especially eaten warm from the pan with a smear of butter or toasted over the fire and topped with peanut butter. Of course, you can always eat it for breakfast, too. This banana bread gets its moist texture by using lots of ripe banana.

½ CUP (1 STICK) UNSALTED BUTTER, AT ROOM TEMPERATURE, PLUS ADDITIONAL FOR PREPARING THE DUTCH OVEN

1 CUP SUGAR

4 LARGE EGGS, LIGHTLY BEATEN

4 LARGE, RIPE BANANAS, MASHED

3 CUPS ALL-PURPOSE FLOUR

1 TABLESPOON BAKING POWDER

¼ TEASPOON KOSHER SALT

1 Coat the Dutch oven lightly with butter.

2 In a medium bowl, stir together the butter and sugar until well combined. Add the eggs and bananas, and stir to mix well. Add the flour, baking powder, and salt, and stir until just mixed.

3 Transfer the batter to the prepared Dutch oven, cover the pot, and set it over a bed of 7 hot coals. Add 16 hot coals on top and bake for about 40 minutes, rotating the pot by a quarter turn every 10 to 15 minutes. Test the bread for doneness using a wooden skewer. Inserted into the center of the bread, it should come out clean when the bread is cooked through. Remove the pot from the heat and let rest for 5 to 10 minutes before serving.

BUTTERY CAMPFIRE BEER BREAD

VEGETARIAN
SOY-FREE
NUT-FREE

SERVES 8

PREP TIME
5 MINUTES, PLUS
20 MINUTES FOR
DOUGH TO RISE

COOK TIME
1 HOUR

21 COALS, PLUS
ADDITIONAL TO
REPLACE COALS AS
THEY BURN OUT

Variation:

The trick here is using self-rising flour, which already has baking powder and salt added to it. If you don't have that, you can substitute 4¼ cups all-purpose flour mixed with 2 tablespoons baking powder and 1 teaspoon salt.

Combining self-rising flour and beer gives you an airy bread without having to bother with yeast or other leavening agents. The beer also adds malty flavor to the bread. Bathed in butter before baking, this bread is tasty enough to eat on its own for a snack but also makes a great side dish for stew, soup, or chili.

6 TABLESPOONS MELTED UNSALTED BUTTER, PLUS ADDITIONAL FOR PREPARING THE DUTCH OVEN

4½ CUPS SELF-RISING FLOUR

5 TABLESPOONS SUGAR

½ TEASPOON KOSHER SALT

1½ (12-OUNCE) CANS OR BOTTLES OF BEER, AT ROOM TEMPERATURE

1 Coat the Dutch oven lightly with butter. Warm the Dutch oven over a bed of 7 hot coals.

2 In a large bowl, mix together the flour, sugar, and salt. Stir in the beer until well incorporated. Remove the Dutch oven from the heat and transfer the dough into it. Cover the pot and let the dough rise for about 20 minutes.

3 Drizzle the melted butter over the top of the dough and cover the pot. Place the Dutch oven over a bed of 7 hot coals and place 14 hot coals on the lid. Rotate the lid by a quarter turn every 10 to 15 minutes and cook for 20 minutes. Take the pot off of the bed of coals, leaving the coals on top, and cook for an additional 40 minutes, until the bread is golden brown. Serve warm or at room temperature.

HONEY-SWEETENED CORNBREAD

VEGETARIAN
SOY-FREE
NUT-FREE

SERVES 8

PREP TIME
5 MINUTES

COOK TIME
25 MINUTES

25 COALS

Variation:
Dress this simple cornbread up by adding a can of cream-style corn, 1½ cups of fresh or frozen corn kernels, 2 or 3 diced jalapeño peppers, or a cup of shredded cheese to the batter.

Cornbread is the perfect accompaniment to any type of chili or barbecue. Cooking it in a cast iron Dutch oven gives it a uniquely crunchy crust that makes it especially good for dunking and soaking up flavorful sauces.

6 TABLESPOONS MELTED BUTTER,
    PLUS ADDITIONAL FOR PREPARING
    THE DUTCH OVEN

1½ CUPS CORNMEAL

1½ CUPS PLUS 1½ TABLESPOONS
    SELF-RISING FLOUR

1 TEASPOON KOSHER SALT

3 LARGE EGGS, BEATEN

1½ CUPS MILK OR BUTTERMILK

½ CUP HONEY

1   Lightly coat the Dutch oven with butter. Preheat the Dutch oven on a bed of 8 hot coals and place 17 hot coals on the lid.

2   In a large bowl, whisk together the cornmeal, flour, and salt. In a medium bowl, whisk the eggs, buttermilk, honey, and melted butter until well combined. Add the egg mixture to the dry ingredients and stir just until combined.

3   Remove the Dutch oven from the heat, remove the lid, and pour the batter into the pan, spreading it out into an even layer with a rubber spatula or the back of a spoon. Replace the lid with the coals on top and return the pot to the heat. Bake for about 25 minutes, until a toothpick inserted into the center comes out clean.

HERBED DINNER ROLLS

VEGETARIAN
SOY-FREE
NUT-FREE

MAKES 16 ROLLS

PREP TIME
10 MINUTES,
PLUS 1 HOUR AND
30 MINUTES FOR
DOUGH TO RISE

COOK TIME
15 MINUTES

26 COALS

Variation:
Sprinkle ½ cup grated
Parmesan cheese over
the dough balls in
the Dutch oven
before baking.

Freshly baked dinner rolls are sure to impress your camping companions. These are laced with Italian herb seasoning, making them extra special and the perfect partner for saucy Italian dishes like Dutch Oven-Baked Eggplant Parmesan (page 83) or Chicken Parmesan (page 101), or for soups like Italian Tomato and Orzo Soup (page 65).

2¾ CUPS ALL-PURPOSE FLOUR, PLUS UP TO ½
    CUP MORE IF NEEDED

¾ CUP SUGAR

¾ TEASPOON KOSHER SALT

2 TABLESPOONS ACTIVE DRY YEAST

6 TABLESPOONS UNSALTED BUTTER, AT
    ROOM TEMPERATURE

⅔ CUP HOT WATER

1 LARGE EGG, BEATEN

1 TABLESPOON ITALIAN SEASONING MIX

COOKING OIL FOR PREPARING THE
    DUTCH OVEN

1   In a large bowl, combine ¾ cup of the flour with the sugar, salt, and yeast. Add the butter and water, and stir until the mixture is well combined. Add the egg, an additional ½ cup of the flour, and the Italian seasoning. Knead the dough with your hands in the bowl, adding the remaining flour about ½ cup at a time, until you have a soft, smooth dough.

2   Form the dough into a ball, cover the bowl, and let the dough rise for about 1 hour, until doubled in size.

3   Coat the Dutch oven lightly with cooking oil and place it over a bed of 10 hot coals. Cover the pot and place 16 hot coals on the lid.

4   Punch down the dough and form it into 16 balls of roughly equal size. Remove the warm Dutch oven from the heat and place the dough balls in a single layer in the bottom. Cover the pot and let the dough rise again until doubled in size, about 30 more minutes.

5   Return the Dutch oven to the bed of 10 hot coals, cover the pot, and place 16 hot coals on the lid. Bake for 10 to 15 minutes, until the rolls are cooked through and golden brown on the outside. Serve warm or at room temperature.

FLUFFY POTATO BREAD

VEGETARIAN
SOY-FREE
NUT-FREE

SERVES 8

PREP TIME
20 MINUTES,
PLUS 1 HOUR AND
40 MINUTES FOR
DOUGH TO RISE

COOK TIME
45 MINUTES

21 COALS

Adding mashed potatoes to your dough adds flavor and makes it super fluffy. This bread is perfect for dunking into soups, stews, and sauces. Because it has a subtle, smoky flavor from being baked over a campfire, it's ideal when paired with your favorite sandwich toppings.

2 CUPS WARM MILK

1 TEASPOON SUGAR

1 PACKET INSTANT YEAST (2¼ TEASPOONS)

1 LARGE POTATO (SUCH AS RUSSET OR IDAHO), COOKED, PEELED, AND MASHED

2 TEASPOONS SALT

2 TABLESPOONS OLIVE OIL, PLUS ADDITIONAL FOR PREPARING THE DUTCH OVEN

4½ TO 5½ CUPS ALL-PURPOSE FLOUR

1   Stir together the milk, sugar, and yeast. Cover and let rest for about 10 minutes, until foamy. Add the potato, salt, and olive oil and stir to mix. Add 1 cup of the flour and stir to incorporate. Add the remaining flour 1 cup at a time until you have added 4 cups. Continue to add flour about ¼ to ½ cup at a time, kneading it in with your hands, until the dough is smooth and springy. The extra cup of flour may not be necessary.

2   Lightly oil a large bowl and place the dough inside. Cover and let rise in a warm spot until doubled in size (about 1 hour). Punch the dough down, cover again, and let rise for 30 more minutes.

3 Lightly oil the Dutch oven and preheat it for about 10 minutes on a bed of 7 hot coals with 14 hot coals on the lid.

4 After the second rise, place the dough in the preheated Dutch oven and make 3 to 4 parallel slits in the top with a sharp knife. Return the Dutch oven to the fire and cover, including the hot coals. Bake the bread for 35 to 45 minutes, until the crust is golden brown. Remove the loaf from the pot and let rest for 10 minutes before slicing. Serve warm or at room temperature.

CRUSTY NO-KNEAD FRENCH BREAD

VEGAN
SOY-FREE
NUT-FREE

SERVES 8

PREP TIME
10 MINUTES, PLUS AT
LEAST 4 HOURS FOR
DOUGH TO RISE

COOK TIME
40 MINUTES

34 COALS

Camp Hack:
If you are letting the
dough rise overnight,
keep it in your tent
where it will be warmer
than outdoors (but
not if you are in bear
country!). Or mix
the dough up at home
and let it rise before
you leave or in the car.

No-knead breads became popular a few years ago because they are so easy to make. Baking them in Dutch ovens makes them especially crusty on the outside, and the high heat makes for a delightfully lofty rise. Use this bread for sandwiches, for dunking into soups and stews, or just for snacking.

3 CUPS BREAD FLOUR, PLUS EXTRA
    FOR DUSTING
½ TEASPOON INSTANT YEAST
1½ TEASPOONS KOSHER SALT
1½ CUPS WARM WATER
COOKING OIL FOR PREPARING THE
    DUTCH OVEN

1   In a large bowl, stir together the flour, yeast, and salt. Stir in the water until a sticky dough forms. Cover the bowl tightly with plastic wrap and set aside to rise, in a warm spot, for a minimum of 4 hours, or up to 20 hours if the air is cool.

2   Lightly coat the Dutch oven with oil and preheat it for at least 15 minutes by placing it on a bed of 12 hot coals with 22 hot coals on the lid.

3 Dust the dough with a little flour and form into a ball. Place the dough into the preheated Dutch oven, replace the lid, including the hot coals, and bake for 30 to 40 minutes, until the dough is nicely browned and crisp.

4 Remove the bread from the Dutch oven and let rest and cool for at least 30 minutes before slicing. Serve warm or at room temperature.

WHOLE WHEAT WALNUT AND CRANBERRY BREAD

VEGAN
SOY-FREE

SERVES 8

PREP TIME
10 MINUTES, PLUS
AT LEAST 4 HOURS
FOR DOUGH TO RISE

COOK TIME
40 MINUTES

34 COALS

This no-knead bread replaces some of the bread flour with whole wheat for extra flavor, texture, and nutrients. Chock-full of cranberries and walnuts, this bread is delicious for breakfast, spread with butter or cream cheese.

2 CUPS BREAD FLOUR, PLUS EXTRA
    FOR DUSTING

1 CUP WHOLE WHEAT FLOUR

½ TEASPOON INSTANT YEAST

½ CUP DRIED CRANBERRIES

½ CUP CHOPPED WALNUTS

1½ TEASPOONS KOSHER SALT

1½ CUPS WARM WATER

OIL FOR PREPARING THE DUTCH OVEN

1   In a large bowl, combine the bread flour, whole wheat flour, yeast, cranberries, walnuts, and salt. Stir in the water until a sticky dough forms. Cover the bowl tightly with plastic wrap and set aside to rise, in a warm spot, for a minimum of 4 hours, or up to 20 hours if the air is cool.

2   Lightly coat the Dutch oven with oil and preheat it for at least 15 minutes by placing it on a bed of 12 hot coals with 22 hot coals on the lid.

3 Dust the dough with a little flour and form it into a ball. Place the dough into the preheated Dutch oven, replace the lid, including the hot coals, and bake for 30 to 40 minutes, until the dough is nicely browned and crisp.

4 Remove the bread from the Dutch oven and let rest and cool for at least 30 minutes before slicing. Serve warm or at room temperature.

ROSEMARY OLIVE OIL BREAD

VEGETARIAN
SOY-FREE
NUT-FREE

SERVES 8

PREP TIME
10 MINUTES, PLUS AT
LEAST 4 HOURS FOR
DOUGH TO RISE

COOK TIME
40 MINUTES

34 COALS

Variation:
To make this bread
even more special, add
¾ cup chopped, pitted
olives along with the
rosemary.

This moist bread gets its tender crumb and loads of flavor from the addition of a bit of olive oil, a dash of vinegar, and a dose of fresh rosemary. It's perfect served alongside One-Pot Spaghetti in Meat Sauce (page 108) or Dutch Oven–Baked Eggplant Parmesan (page 83).

3 CUPS BREAD FLOUR

½ TEASPOON INSTANT YEAST

1½ TEASPOONS KOSHER SALT

¼ TEASPOON VINEGAR (ANY TYPE
  YOU PREFER)

2 TABLESPOONS CHOPPED FRESH ROSEMARY

1¼ CUPS WARM WATER

¼ CUP EXTRA VIRGIN OLIVE OIL, PLUS
  ADDITIONAL FOR PREPARING THE
  DUTCH OVEN

1   In a large bowl, stir together the flour, yeast, salt, vinegar, and rosemary. Stir in the warm water and olive oil, and mix until a sticky dough forms.

2   Cover the bowl tightly with plastic wrap and set aside to rise, in a warm spot, for a minimum of 4 hours, or up to 20 hours if the air is cool.

3   Lightly coat the Dutch oven with oil and preheat it for at least 15 minutes by placing it on a bed of 12 hot coals with 22 hot coals on the lid.

4   Dust the dough with a little flour and form into a ball. Place the dough into the preheated Dutch oven, replace the lid, including the hot coals, and bake for 30 to 40 minutes, until the dough is nicely browned and crisp.

5   Remove the bread from the Dutch oven and let rest and cool for at least 30 minutes before slicing. Serve warm or at room temperature.

Chapter
Eight

Desserts

BROWN SUGAR BERRY CRISP

VEGETARIAN
SOY-FREE
NUT-FREE

SERVES 6

PREP TIME
5 MINUTES

COOK TIME
30 MINUTES

28 COALS

Seasonal Swap:

This crisp is delicious with other fruits added to the mix. I like a combination of peaches or nectarines with blackberries or blueberries. In the fall, apple or pear also work well.

A mixture of sweet berries and brown sugar cooks down to syrupy goodness, and a toasted topping of oats and brown sugar adds just the right touch of crunchiness. Serve this with a dollop of sweetened whipped cream (I like to bring along an all-natural canned version) or vanilla yogurt.

COOKING OIL TO PREPARE THE DUTCH OVEN

6 CUPS FRESH BERRIES (BLUEBERRIES, BLACKBERRIES, STRAWBERRIES, RASPBERRIES, OR A COMBINATION)

½ CUP PLUS ⅓ CUP LIGHT BROWN SUGAR, DIVIDED

2 TABLESPOONS WATER

2 TABLESPOONS CORNSTARCH

½ CUP UNCOOKED OATS

¼ CUP ALL-PURPOSE FLOUR

½ CUP (1 STICK) UNSALTED BUTTER, MELTED

1 Lightly oil the Dutch oven.

2 In the Dutch oven, toss together the berries, ⅓ cup of the brown sugar, water, and cornstarch.

3 In a small bowl, stir together the oats, flour, the remaining ½ cup of brown sugar, and butter. Sprinkle the oat mixture evenly over the berries. Cover the Dutch oven with the lid.

4 Set the Dutch oven over a bed of 7 hot coals, cover, and place 21 hot coals on the lid. Bake for 25 to 30 minutes, until the fruit is bubbling and the topping is golden brown. Serve warm.

GOOEY CARAMEL BAKED APPLES

VEGETARIAN
SOY-FREE
NUT-FREE

SERVES 8

PREP TIME
10 MINUTES

COOK TIME
45 MINUTES

26 COALS

Placing a caramel in the center of each apple half before baking is a stroke of genius. The candy melts into a delectable pool that oozes over the apple when you cut into it. A brown sugar and cinnamon topping adds flavor and even more oozy goodness.

4 LARGE, CRISP APPLES

4 CARAMELS

3 TABLESPOONS UNSALTED BUTTER, MELTED

¼ CUP (PACKED) BROWN SUGAR

1½ TABLESPOONS ALL-PURPOSE FLOUR

1½ TEASPOONS CINNAMON

1   Cut the apples in half and scoop out the core from each half using a small metal spoon. Cut 2 concentric circles into the apple halves around the scooped-out centers. Turn the apples over and make several slits without cutting through the center of the apple.

2   Arrange the apple halves in the Dutch oven, cut side up. Place a caramel into the center of each apple half.

3   In a small bowl, stir together the butter, brown sugar, flour, and cinnamon. Spoon this mixture over the apple halves in the Dutch oven, dividing evenly. Place the lid on the Dutch oven.

4   Place the Dutch oven over a bed of 6 hot coals and place 20 hot coals on the lid. Bake for 35 to 45 minutes, until the apples are tender. Serve warm.

NUTTY SALTED CARAMEL POPCORN

VEGETARIAN
GLUTEN-FREE
SOY-FREE

SERVES 6

PREP TIME
5 MINUTES

COOK TIME
5 MINUTES

15 COALS

Making caramel popcorn is much easier you think, and the Dutch oven is the perfect vessel for it. You just melt butter and brown sugar into a syrupy caramel sauce, then toss in popcorn and peanuts. The kosher salt and salty peanuts balance the sweetness of the caramel.

1 CUP (2 STICKS) UNSALTED BUTTER
1¼ CUPS BROWN SUGAR
½ CUP CORN SYRUP
½ TEASPOON KOSHER SALT
6 CUPS POPPED POPCORN
½ CUP CHOPPED SALTED PEANUTS

1 Place the Dutch oven over a bed of 15 hot coals. Add the butter, brown sugar, corn syrup, and salt, and cook. Stir until the butter melts and the mixture thickens and darkens a bit.

2 Remove the Dutch oven from the heat and stir in the popcorn and peanuts until well coated. Transfer the mixture in heaping spoonfuls to wax paper and let cool before serving.

QUICK AND EASY PEACH PIE

VEGETARIAN
SOY-FREE
NUT-FREE

SERVES 8

PREP TIME
10 MINUTES, PLUS
1 HOUR FOR PIE TO
COOL

COOK TIME
40 MINUTES

26 COALS

Camp Hack:

You can make your own piecrust, but the simplest way to make this is to buy a prepared, refrigerated piecrust in an aluminum foil tin. Alternatively, you can make a crust from scratch at home, press it into a disposable aluminum pie tin, freeze it, and then stash it in your cooler.

Nothing beats a pie made from fresh peaches on a summer evening in the great outdoors. Using a prepared piecrust (either store-bought or one you've premade at home) makes this recipe a snap to make at your campsite.

1 (9-INCH) PREPARED PIECRUST

¾ CUP SUGAR

2 TABLESPOONS UNSALTED BUTTER, AT ROOM TEMPERATURE

⅓ CUP ALL-PURPOSE FLOUR

¼ TEASPOON GROUND NUTMEG

6 PEACHES, PEELED, PITTED, AND SLICED

1   If using a flat piecrust, press it into the bottom and up the sides of an aluminum pie tin (be sure the pie tin will fit in the Dutch oven). Crimp the edges, cutting off any excess.

2   In a medium bowl, stir together the sugar and butter to mix well. Stir in the flour and nutmeg, and mix until it resembles a coarse meal. Spread half of this flour mixture over the bottom of the piecrust. Arrange the peach slices over the top of the butter-flour mixture, overlapping them as needed, and then sprinkle the remaining butter-flour mixture over the top. Place the pie in the Dutch oven and cover with the lid.

3   Set the Dutch oven on a bed of 6 hot coals and place 20 hot coals on the lid. Bake for about 40 minutes, until the crust is browned and the filling is bubbling. Remove the Dutch oven from the heat and let the pie cool for at least an hour before serving.

DOUBLE-CRUST CINNAMON APPLE PIE

VEGETARIAN
SOY-FREE
NUT-FREE

SERVES 8

PREP TIME
10 MINUTES

COOK TIME
50 MINUTES

26 COALS

Variation:
Add 6 to 8 chopped caramels to the filling before placing it in the crust to make this into a caramel apple pie.

Crisp apples are delicious and travel well, but sometimes you want to dress them up a bit. This simple double-crusted pie is an easy way to do just that. Using premade or store-bought piecrusts makes this recipe camp kitchen friendly.

2 (9-INCH) PREPARED PIECRUSTS
6 APPLES, PEELED, CORED, AND THINLY SLICED
¾ CUP SUGAR
2 TABLESPOONS ALL-PURPOSE FLOUR
¾ TEASPOON GROUND CINNAMON
¼ TEASPOON SALT

1 Press one of the piecrusts into the bottom and up the sides of an aluminum pie tin (be sure the pie tin will fit in the Dutch oven). Crimp the edges, cutting off any excess.

2 In a large bowl, stir together the apples, sugar, flour, cinnamon, and salt. Transfer the mixture to the piecrust in the tin, spreading the apple slices out into an even layer. Top with the remaining piecrust, crimping it around the edges and cutting off any overhang. Make several slits in the top crust to allow steam to escape. Place the pie in the Dutch oven and cover with the lid.

3 Set the Dutch oven on a bed of 6 hot coals and place 20 hot coals on the lid. Bake for 45 to 50 minutes, until the crust is browned and the filling is bubbling. Remove the Dutch oven from the heat and let the pie cool for at least an hour before serving.

SUNNY ORANGE CAKE

VEGETARIAN
SOY-FREE
NUT-FREE

SERVES 8 TO 10

PREP TIME
10 MINUTES

COOK TIME
40 MINUTES

24 COALS

Variation:

Add an ooey, gooey coconut topping to make this cake even more special. Melt ¼ cup unsalted butter in a small saucepan. Combine ½ cup plus 2 tablespoons brown sugar, ¼ cup milk, and 1 cup shredded unsweetened coconut and stir to mix well. Pour the topping over the cake when it is finished baking, replace the lid, and cook for about 5 minutes longer, until the topping is bubbling.

Orange zest and orange juice flavor this simple white cake. For a tart lemon cake, you can substitute an equal quantity of lemon zest and lemon juice, or use a mix of both orange and lemon if you like. Serve this cake with whipped cream and fresh berries or other fruit on top if you're feeling fancy.

2 TABLESPOONS MELTED UNSALTED BUTTER, PLUS ADDITIONAL FOR PREPARING THE DUTCH OVEN

4 LARGE EGGS, BEATEN

2 CUPS SUGAR

2 CUPS SELF-RISING FLOUR

FRESHLY GRATED ZEST OF 1 LARGE ORANGE

¼ CUP FRESHLY SQUEEZED ORANGE JUICE

¾ CUP MILK

1 Lightly coat the Dutch oven with butter.

2 Whisk the eggs until they are frothy and then whisk in the sugar. Add the flour and stir to mix well. Stir in the orange zest, orange juice, milk, and butter.

3 Transfer the batter to the prepared Dutch oven and cover with the lid.

4 Set the Dutch oven over a bed of 6 hot coals and place 18 hot coals on the lid. Bake for 35 to 40 minutes, until a wooden skewer or toothpick inserted into the center of the cake comes out clean.

PINEAPPLE UPSIDE-DOWN CAKE

VEGETARIAN
SOY-FREE
NUT-FREE

SERVES 8

PREP TIME
10 MINUTES

COOK TIME
25 MINUTES

23 COALS

Camp Hack:
To make it easier to get the cake out of the pot—and to make cleanup easier—line the Dutch oven with heavy-duty aluminum foil before adding the butter and brown sugar.

Pineapple upside-down cake is a classic, and the Dutch oven is a great way to cook it. The high, even heat of the pot gives the cake a spectacularly caramelized topping. It's also easy to make with pantry items, including a can of pineapple rings, but you can always substitute fresh pineapple if you've got it, fresh peaches, nectarines, blackberries, or a combination.

1 CUP (2 STICKS) UNSALTED BUTTER, AT
　　ROOM TEMPERATURE, DIVIDED

¾ CUP WHITE SUGAR

2 LARGE EGGS, BEATEN

2 CUPS SELF-RISING FLOUR

1 CAN SLICED PINEAPPLE RINGS IN JUICE,
　　DRAINED, ½ CUP OF THE JUICE RESERVED

¼ CUP BROWN SUGAR

1　In a large bowl, combine ¾ cup (1½ sticks) of the butter with the sugar and stir until well combined and creamy. Add the eggs and mix until incorporated. Add the flour and stir to combine. Stir in the reserved pineapple juice.

2　Place the Dutch oven over a bed of 8 hot coals. Add the remaining ¼ cup of butter and the brown sugar to the pot and cook, stirring frequently, until the mixture bubbles and darkens a bit, about 3 minutes.

3 Remove the pot from the heat and spread the butter and brown sugar mixture out evenly over the bottom of the Dutch oven and arrange the pineapple rings in a single layer on top. Pour the cake batter over the pineapple and place the lid on the pot. Return the pot to the heat.

4 Place 15 hot coals on the lid of the Dutch oven. Bake for about 20 minutes and then check for doneness (a wooden skewer or toothpick inserted into the center will come out clean). Continue to cook, if necessary, checking every few minutes until done.

5 Remove the pot from the heat and let cool for about 5 minutes. Place a large plate on top of the pot and invert the pot (carefully, with heat-proof gloves protecting your hands and forearms) so that the cake releases onto the plate. Serve warm or at room temperature.

BUTTERMILK CHOCOLATE CAKE

VEGETARIAN
SOY-FREE
NUT-FREE

SERVES 8

PREP TIME
10 MINUTES

COOK TIME
50 MINUTES

24 COALS

Variation:
If you don't have buttermilk, you can substitute sour cream or plain yogurt thinned with a little milk, or regular milk "acidified" by adding a tablespoon of vinegar or lemon juice to a cup of regular milk.

This rich chocolate cake couldn't be easier to make. Buttermilk makes it super moist and flavorful. You can top it with fresh fruit, whipped cream, or non-dairy whipped topping, but it is also scrumptious eaten plain while it's still warm.

1 CUP COOKING OIL, PLUS ADDITIONAL FOR PREPARING THE DUTCH OVEN

1 CUP BUTTERMILK

2 LARGE EGGS, BEATEN

2 CUPS SELF-RISING FLOUR

2 CUPS SUGAR

¾ CUP UNSWEETENED COCOA POWDER

1 CUP BOILING WATER

1 Lightly oil the Dutch oven with cooking oil.

2 In a large bowl, whisk together the oil, buttermilk, and eggs.

3 In a separate bowl, combine the flour, sugar, and cocoa. Mix to combine well.

4 Add the dry ingredients gradually to the wet ingredients, whisking until the batter is smooth. Stir in the boiling water.

5 Transfer the batter to the Dutch oven and cover with the lid.

6 Place the Dutch oven on a bed of 8 hot coals and place 16 hot coals on the lid. Bake for 45 to 50 minutes, until a wooden skewer or toothpick inserted into the center of the cake comes out clean.

DOUBLE-CHOCOLATE BROWNIES

VEGETARIAN
SOY-FREE
NUT-FREE

SERVES 8 TO 10

PREP TIME
5 MINUTES

COOK TIME
30 MINUTES

28 COALS

Variation:
Add a cup of chopped walnuts along with the chocolate chips, if desired.

Indoors or out, rich chocolate brownies are always a treat. These get chocolate flavor from both cocoa powder and chocolate chips. The batter takes only a few minutes to mix up, and the Dutch oven bakes them to perfection with a crunchy outer crust and gooey center.

¾ CUP (1½ STICKS) UNSALTED BUTTER,
    MELTED, PLUS ADDITIONAL FOR PREPARING
    THE DUTCH OVEN

¾ CUP ALL-PURPOSE FLOUR

1½ CUPS SUGAR

½ CUP COCOA POWDER

¼ TEASPOON KOSHER SALT

3 LARGE EGGS, BEATEN

1 CUP SEMISWEET CHOCOLATE CHIPS

1   Lightly coat the Dutch oven with butter.

2   In a medium bowl, mix together the flour, sugar, cocoa powder, and salt. In a small bowl, whisk the melted butter and eggs together. Add the egg mixture to the dry ingredients and stir to combine. Stir in the chocolate chips. Pour the batter into the prepared Dutch oven and cover with the lid.

3   Place the Dutch oven on a bed of 10 hot coals and place 18 hot coals on the lid. Bake for 20 minutes and then check to see if the brownies are done (a wooden skewer or toothpick inserted into the center will come out clean). If necessary, continue cooking, checking every 3 to 5 minutes, until done. Remove the Dutch oven from the heat and let the brownies cool for 10 to 15 minutes before cutting into squares and serving.

DUTCH OVEN LAYERED BANANA S'MORES PIE

SOY-FREE
NUT-FREE

SERVES 8

PREP TIME
10 MINUTES

COOK TIME
20 MINUTES

24 COALS

Because you can't have a camping cookbook without a recipe that combines crunchy graham crackers, gooey marshmallows, and melted chocolate, I give you this recipe for a s'mores pie made in the Dutch oven. A layer of sweetened condensed milk gives the pie a gooey, caramelized base. Feel free to substitute or add additional ingredients. Peanut butter chips, toffee chips, shredded coconut, or nuts will only add to the deliciousness. Plus, you won't end up with sticky marshmallow all over your fingers.

1 (14 OUNCE) CAN SWEETENED CONDENSED MILK

1 PREMADE GRAHAM CRACKER CRUMB PIECRUST IN A DISPOSABLE ALUMINUM TIN

2 LARGE, RIPE BANANAS, SLICED

2 CUPS CHOCOLATE CHIPS

2 CUPS MINI MARSHMALLOWS

1   Pour the sweetened condensed milk over the graham cracker crust (be sure the pie tin will fit inside the Dutch oven). Arrange the banana slices in a single layer over the milk. Sprinkle the chocolate chips over the bananas in an even layer. Top with the marshmallows.

2   Place the pie tin into the Dutch oven and place the lid on the pot. Set the Dutch oven on a bed of 6 hot coals and place 18 hot coals on the lid. Bake for about 20 minutes, until the chocolate has melted and the marshmallows are golden brown on top.

Essential Technique:

You can make your own graham cracker crumb crust—either at home before you go or at camp—by combining 2 cups graham cracker crumbs with a ½ cup of melted butter. Press the mixture into a disposable aluminum pie tin (be sure the pie tin will fit inside the Dutch oven).

Conversion Tables

Volume Equivalents (Dry)

US STANDARD	METRIC (APPROXIMATE)
⅛ teaspoon	0.5 mL
¼ teaspoon	1 mL
½ teaspoon	2 mL
¾ teaspoon	4 mL
1 teaspoon	5 mL
1 tablespoon	15 mL
¼ cup	59 mL
⅓ cup	79 mL
½ cup	118 mL
⅔ cup	156 mL
¾ cup	177 mL
1 cup	235 mL
2 cups or 1 pint	475 mL
3 cups	700 mL
4 cups or 1 quart	1 L
½ gallon	2 L
1 gallon	4 L

Volume Equivalents (Liquid)

US STANDARD	US STANDARD (OUNCES)	METRIC (APPROXIMATE)
2 tablespoons	1 fl. oz.	30 mL
¼ cup	2 fl. oz.	60 mL
½ cup	4 fl. oz.	120 mL
1 cup	8 fl. oz.	240 mL
1½ cups	12 fl. oz.	355 mL
2 cups or 1 pint	16 fl. oz.	475 mL
4 cups or 1 quart	32 fl. oz.	1 L
1 gallon	128 fl. oz.	4 L

Oven Temperatures

FAHRENHEIT (F)	CELSIUS (C) (APPROXIMATE)
250°F	120°C
300°F	150°C
325°F	165°C
350°F	180°C
375°F	190°C
400°F	200°C
425°F	220°C
450°F	230°C

Recipe Index

Index